VIOLENCE
IN
HEAVEN

VIOLENCE
IN
HEAVEN

Meeting **GOD** Where Rubber Meets the Road

Vincent Brechtel

978-1-965552-54-4 (Paperback)

admin@bookwrightshouse.com
☎ (213) 286 6700

Table of Contents

EPIGRAPH

Birth is violent, whether in an instant Creation births a universe, a baby struggles towards its first breath or the smallest tree bursts from the confines of its seed shell. Yes birth is violent but the only moment where violence ever need be necessary within life. Rather life but only be expectant, energetic and carefully tender as it awaits the excitement of the emergence of its blossoms, the hopeful self-planting of fruit and the eventual satisfaction of observing one's own seed growing and continuing the honored role of ever better life. Our Creator is mindful of this behavior even as He portrays Life throughout seasons ...

"When its branch has already become tender and puts forth leaves, you know the summer is near"

This book illustrates a certain desire of Provision and announces an approaching season by sharing explicit, encouraging hints from Heaven ... listen carefully people ... God (Love) is this book's main author ... but then decide for yourself based upon what you are willing to believe ... after all, God is the original author of choice and freedom ...

'We the People' whom declare "In God we Trust" have a God who continues to offer help ... especially at this hour of juncture ... He offers guidance towards a clarification of 'seasons' to either help us prepare for either an anticipated approaching season or the somber closing of a door. More specifically He is asking us (Mankind) "What do you want?"

because He is reasonable yet He is certainly 'just'…is yet evaluating our fruit…not particularly happy…but nonetheless asking "What do you want?"…are we willing to stand with Him or are we just too tired to continue…'fall' is a season of either replanting fruit or chopping the tree and burning it…Therefore let us ask ourselves…what do we want…?

Ok then 'We the People' who share the desire of a next season are well to reply "We desire God's will to be done here on Earth!" and then full heartedly help replant.

As we look up to our Father in Heaven with great expectation, let us ponder upon what we know:

"God is Love"

Love: Fruitful unbridled desire for 'Life'

Life: Companionship (Work/Dance) with 'Love'

"Love provides **Life** in abun**dance**"

…and we realize that 'We' (God and Man)…yes God and man…are expected to work together…and that Love is remains patient despite the tedious but temper-able natural spirit of man…Wisdom has patient hands…while we can yet be found workable…

"Behold, I have created the blacksmith who blows the coals in the fire, who brings forth an instrument for his work"

"The Master Craftsman is the Wisdom of God"… "The Master Craftsman delights in the sons of men"

This book is truly a reflection of the Master Craftsman's work of Love and Life in Dance. It is an example of how God breathes Life into all forms of men, so that we might be called by our Father in Heaven, "sons".

These pages provide a witness recount, of God working/dancing with men, through an example of a common man named Aspot. Indeed many people will say these stories are fantastical. Yet no person can affect truth of any moment already gone past and therefore the stories recorded here will ever remain truthful real life interactions with God regardless of how any person, society or education system tries to alter or redefine truth through the application of 'political correctness'. Ignorance can be easily changed but contempt cannot. Faith allows believing in God and that He can be found, very present, in our lives, providing better insight into His heart (Wisdom).

The man called Aspot is so named because he has proven himself to be problematic and blemished. Yet for all practical purposes, Aspot is only a placeholder for, this moment, as God discusses with you the Reader ... perhaps you are of a kind ... a person whom can satisfy Love (God) as He and you work together ... fruitfully ... building Life ...

ACKNOWLEDGING

My granddaughter and every child maimed through prideful ignorance

1

INTO AN ORE FURNACE

Journey Begins

His forehead stings from the latest outburst of the sky and he squints to help see the outlines of the road blurred by the rapidly descending deluge of rain and sleet. It is mid-afternoon of what has been an intermittently wet and chilly September day. His spirit is as dark as the demons he can feel riding on his shoulders and even now gnawing at his heel.

In the distance, is seen, an interstate overpass approaching which is about the only thing, he considers good this entire ride. But he wonders if his motorcycle is even going to make it that far. Indeed the engine is sporadically coughing loudly and issuing weak backfire while climbing a small knoll towards the concrete crossroad overpass located in a barren landscape somewhere within the middle of Montana.

As if obligingly to a disgusted kick, his bike whines and complains but also chugs contemptuously under this concrete umbrella. "Whew!" Aspot quietly mutters "I didn't think you were going to make it you stupid ole nag" as he allows the old bagger to throat a dying cough and quietly roll to a stop even as it proceeds to muddle the roadside with puddles of oil and rain water.

Slowly and a bit stiffly he lifts himself from the seat and steps back far enough to cast an angry eye at this thing which is proving itself to be about as worthless as his repeatedly unfaithful wife. For a moment he is tempted to just kick that bike over and thumb it the remainder of the trip, which is to spend some time with his brother living near Seattle. Rather he only grunts and scrambles up a steep embankment to sit on a ledge of a concrete shoulder near the bottom side of the overpass, somewhat out of the wind. He leans back against a concrete abutment and glares down at his bike wondering just how much worse things can get.

None of his efforts to save his marriage seemed good enough and very recently his wife let him know that her latest fling (boyfriend) is so important this time, that she "no longer needs" Aspot and it is simply best if he packs his bags and goes anywhere far away. But of course she also made it very clear that he had still better expect to pay child-support because she is going to ask the court for the family home he built and to continue supporting her.

Yes, his wife has long been faithless to her entire family, at times disappearing for days then later showing back up with no sense of remorse and acting as if nothing is amiss, but certain to show contempt and anger if questioned. Aspot at first hoped she was just taking innocent and needed time away. But when she had once quietly handed him a bottle of prescribed pills needed to cure a venereal disease, most certainly already passed to him, the foreshadow of what was to follow, the inherent challenge,

2

of keeping his family intact dismally increased in attitude and somberly in prayer. But to no avail, because the past two years she has been coming home increasing later, at times not until after the sun is far past being back up. He had to stop handing her his paycheck and take charge of paying the family bills, so that they actually got paid.

But at this moment, Aspot is distant, cold, wet and altogether miserable as he dismally ponders what the "slow train" has brought. He has quietly accepted her dismissal of him and summarily resigned from a long-term job. And then, with no plan in hand, tied his sleeping bag to the handlebars, inventoried the tools in his saddlebags and stuffed in a dozen pair of clean socks.

Then he had sat in the middle of the couch and called his three children from their rooms to come sit with him. He kept his talk with them short by only letting them know that he is no longer employed and is going to be gone for a while as he looks for work. But that he loves them, will be missing them and to expect him writing often (which he did). He smiles, now in the shadow of the overpass, as he ponders how they had all looked at him with sincere concern and love and grabbed tightly onto his waist while he wrapped them in his arms for a great big hug, then kissed each with love on the cheek and captured the unique smell of each before getting up and quickly saying goodbye.

They did not need to know what was fully happening yet. Besides he didn't know either and definitely did not know how to better explain. Anyway they will figure it out very shortly when a strange man's face shows up at their breakfast table. The oldest daughter is still only a young teenager but Aspot is confident that she is also sensible enough to take care of her brother and sister much better than her mother has ever been able.

Rain and sleet are now blowing hard against his bike below and tugging at his wet pant leg. Sigh, somehow life has remained very disordered and chaotic no matter how hard he has tried. When he had married it was in his heart to be a faithful husband and father. He has always remained employed, found pleasure in pleasing his wife and attending school affairs and t-ball games of his children. And even when it became obvious in many ways, that his wife had little interest in any part of Life with him, he continued to look for ways to please her. And at times it even seemed like there might be hope on the horizon. But such times only lasted but for a moment.

He considers many things as he listens to the rain splatter on the above concrete lid and a distant crack of thunder. "Just what has happened and what have I done wrong?" he questions himself. "Where is that god I have wasted so much time going to church for?" he angrily mocks. Yes, he has always maintained a habit of regular church attendance of the faith he was born into. His children always went to Sunday services with him although his wife rarely did. Yes, over the years he has had brief encounters with situations that suggested God might very well be present. But, now in his mind, all of those brief "God" experiences could have only been but desperate thoughts with hope for encouragement.

After nearly an hour of many dark thoughts and glaring down, at that ill-running motorcycle, he feels as if very near the brink. He just wants give up on everything including even anger. Nothing good could be seen anywhere on the horizon. In his mind, both he and "that god" are total failures. "I am done!" he mutters angrily while making a grim somber decision to go kick over that worthless bike, retrieve his sleeping bag and let his two feet carry him down the ever meaningless dark dreary road.

So in a rash moment of anger he grabs hold of the top edge of the incline and with a strong heave drags himself recklessly forward from the abutment in a hopeless, meaningless motion ... but then abruptly stops as his nose brushes some unknown object. He sits back and focuses upon what his nose just encountered and instantly God opens his eyes.

In a single breath his attention and thoughts are thoroughly transformed as he sits back in bewilderment and awe to stare at this object hanging right in front of him. It is dangling from a piece of old boot lace not more than fifteen inches directly in front of his nose. He asks himself "How did I not see this thing, even as I sat here looking directly past it, while glaring at my bike?" "How did I not see it as I had climbed up towards and sat down behind it?" "How is it possible I did not see this cross?"

It is indeed a cross shaped out of what looks like an old piece of once used blasting wire neatly formed about four inches tall and three inches wide, hanging from an old worn boot lace, directly in front of him, between two overpass girders he has been sitting between and under. He is profoundly amazed by how he did not notice this cross hanging directly in front of him until now which is after nearly an hour of sitting. After all, it is certainly suspended directly in line between his eyes and his bike. He ponders this cross and what its mysterious appearance might mean. He feels electricity running up his spine and across his scalp and begins to shake. The corners of his eyes became moist as God then speaks into his heart. He sits there and absorbs Love ... Oh he feels it soaking into him ... the love of God.

He sits silently pondering this Cross and softly cries but not just sure why. In part he weeps with joy feeling the incredible warmth from God. And he cries out of selfish misery, the way a long suppression of pain is allowing, if not begging, him to do. Intense emotion, spins within him like a whirlwind and he reels with an intense feeling of unbalanced vertigo, as if being suddenly caught standing with two feet on different ledges contending against each other above an unfathomable depth. And unable to comprehend the magnitude of contrast between the two ledges and feeling trapped by not knowing how to get both feet onto one side without plummeting into the impenetrable darkness. Yet, like a lost child, he feels the warm embrace of God (Love) and closes his eyes to sob with a deep sense of relief and security.

Almost at the same time the wind quiets, the rain stops and the sun steps from behind the clouds. It is quickly bright outside the overpass and warmth from the low hanging sun feels wonderful upon his skin. Leaning forward he takes hold of that Cross, brings his lips to meet and kiss it. Then he allows the cross to remain, so that another stranger might also be likewise touched, as he scrambles down towards that actually rather handsome old clunker of a motorcycle.

His saddlebags are full of many tools and it does not take long to find the engine troubles are being caused by excessively tight exhaust valves. Remembering the joyful spirit of his dad when whistling, he imitates that joy and expresses a tune through pursed lips while adjusting valves. After a quick adjustment he pulls on his gloves, kicks the engine to life and singing a simple hymn then sets straight towards his new well defined goal. He is now on the road towards finding this Mysterious and Loving God that has greatly and wonderfully surprised him.

He has been given or perhaps rediscovered a security he had possessed in innocence when a boy full of trust, joy and hope. *The picture of that cross hanging from the overpass is now indelibly imprinted in his memory. He is beginning to discover his part of the song and has entered the Dance.*

In fact the rest of this journey, even though this old engine is slowly dying as the exhaust valves, designed for leaded gas, but now burning the recently new unleaded fuel, are rapidly deteriorating. Meanwhile he is still travelling and although needing to repeatedly readjust the valves he remains filled with song as he watches, in awe, the beauty and wonder of God's creation. This trip which began in sadness has unexpectedly become hope filled joy and a progress mark for the beginning of Life.

Many things happened in the following years, some far too bizarre to attempt describing in less words than another entire book could afford. It has now been numerous years, since Aspot first started his search for God and walked through a season of his Life that he sometimes calls "A time in Hell". The Craftsman grins and says "It was only a little time needed within a furnace".

Journey Continues

But as we continue, Aspot claims, it took a long time to get any traction, with Life, because it is difficult to walk in this world without many missteps. The Craftsman wipes dust off his hands, shakes His head and says "No", "Rather creating quality takes time when there is little room for Carbon (The Word) while excessive impurities continue to burn out."

Aspot's oldest daughter is now in high school and living near him in Washington State with a friend of hers, another girl and her family. This seems to be a great arrangement because his daughter is excelling in school and excited about the future. However, Aspot hears from his son, now living in Colorado, that his youngest daughter, who only fourteen years old, has been kicked out of her mother's house. His son reports that his mother piled this sister's clothes on the lawn and locked the door. This happened two weeks earlier and since that time, his son has not seen his sister but his sister's clothes have been moved, by the mother, to the back lawn, to be scattered by dogs amongst much excrement.

Because of being unable to remotely find anyone who might know where his daughter might be Aspot is prompted to resign a well-loved job, pack his possessions in his jeep, kiss his oldest daughter goodbye and head to Colorado where he intends to locate his youngest daughter.

It takes a couple weeks but he does find her and is much relieved to discover that she had been noticed, living on the street, by another girl, her age, who had invited her home for dinner at a nearby but somewhat isolated farm, where she remained. Dear Lord, continue to bless that God filled family!

Soon Aspot is re-employed and his youngest daughter is living with him. Instead of hiking in the Cascades, he hikes the Rockies. Instead of riding the east slope river valley and through aromatic fields of cultivated hops he rides the west slope and through bright blossoms of peach and apple orchards.

Also importantly, within a pocket of his leather jacket is a pocket sized New Testament, Psalms and Proverbs which a kind hearted Gideon handed to him during his most recent Seattle weekend jail cell excursion (Don't read too much into this. Remember the Craftsman was there with him all through his time, there, in the furnace). This book of Holy Scripture gets much attention and is always a perfect reason to take breaks during a ride and stretch his legs while enjoying the sunshine, beauty and solid ground.

One Sunday morning as parishioners of a church, he is now an active participant, crowd out the doors and into the sunshine where he finally meets a friendly woman, whom he has been exchanging glances with for some time now. They engage in a pleasant chat and walk down the lazy street sidewalk, into a local café, to continue talking over a cup of coffee. Again the following Sunday they meet and enjoy a lighthearted brunch in a similar manner. During their third meeting he suggests they take advantage of the much melting mountain snow and brave a whitewater rafting adventure down the Arkansas River canyon. "Ok, I am in!" she says. He obtains tickets and Thursday he calls her to make travel arrangements with her. However, silence is caused for a few moments when she asks if it is ok if her boyfriend comes along.

Whew, this is the first time she had thought to let him know she was dating another man and it is rather disappointing news. Sigh, with an awkward chuckle "Sure it will be fun" he says but now suggests that they meet independently, at the rafting start point, alongside the river.

The following week, the weather is absolutely beautiful and so he takes time off from work that proceeding Friday and enjoys a delightful spring bike excursion through the mountains with intent to camp that night somewhere close to the Arkansas River. As the sun approaches the west horizon he spots a promising side dirt road off the highway and soon finds a lovely remote place to cast his tent. He has that faithful Gideon companion in the pocket of his jacket, comfortably reclines against a large smooth faced chunk of sun-warmed granite and reads.

As he reads he feels deeply moved and cries out "Lord, this is good!", "It makes me wish that I could find time, to read Your Word, more often!" Following this outcry his eyes return to the page but is soon startled when he seems to audibly hear, "I will give you time"

He jumps up and scans all around to find who had spoken but he is in a remote meadow with trees at least two hundred yards distant and can only see much grass and mountain flowers. Upon verifying how far apart he is from everyone he realizes the presence of the Lord and so as his neck and scalp hair crawl he falls to his knees and is silent for minutes. Not hearing anything further he replies, "Thank you." even while considering that this promise is likely to come in accompaniment with some form of discomfort. Nevertheless, certain of the promise and the presence of God he feels greatly blessed.

The following whitewater adventure is memorable although he is a tad bit punchy with that woman and her boyfriend. But God is silently working with both his attitude and his many other flaws.

The promise heard in the mountain meadow does not take long to arrive as Aspot rides past a tawdry dark bar filled with alcohol, smoke and girls that make a living by stripping in public. A demon on his shoulder shouts "Hey look, two dollar beers!", "Besides, it has been so long since you have been with a woman I bet you can't even be aroused anymore" Aspot feeling challenged spins his bike around and steps into that joint. It took a few moments for his eyes to adjust and sure enough there is a stage in the center of this place, but feeling rather uncomfortable he is not yet willing to look above the stage or even that direction. Rather he proceeds directly to the bar, purchases a cheap beer and locates an isolated table in a far corner.

Sitting down he now focuses on the stage just in time to watch a girl strip her last tiny bit of clothing. Immediately he is overcome with embarrassment and moves his chair around to the opposite side of the table so that he can only see but a dingy gray wall to finish his beer and leave. His eyes are closed when he feel a hand run across his shoulder and slide down his arm. "Hey big guy, want a table dance?" He looks up into the eyes of a pretty woman, who, thankfully, is sufficiently covered. "No" he responds.

"Are you so sure" she asks with a grin and a little shake of her tassels. He gazes into her eyes and identifies a form of loneliness little different from his, "Tell you what" he says "Sit and talk to me for ten minutes and I will leave you a Jackson note." "Ok" she says and pulls a chair over to sit across that small table from him then one at a time plies back his fingers from the beer mug until she takes a hold of his entire hand and asks. "So stud just what do you want to talk about?"

"Oh, I don't know. Let's talk about you" then going straight for the jugular he asks "Why do you work here?" With a sudden jerk she pulls her hands back from his, leans back shows a moment of defiance, then looks in his eyes and senses that he is asking from a sincere interest. Her posture softens and her shoulders slump so that he can now also see a certain weariness, which makes her look much older than she really is, as she says "Tell you what" "You can keep your Jackson but I do need a drink to answer what you ask"

They talked honestly for over an hour, he hears that she wants to be a nurse but has a daughter to feed, rent to pay, etc. and has not found a way to get the needed schooling. He confides his hope to find and purchase a mountain property conveniently close enough to build a cabin and allow the daily commute to work. Upon hearing this she slides a calling card, of her realtor friend, across the table to him. Then while preparing to leave, never expecting to see that woman again he says "I kind of think that if you take time to find a church and you will also find a way to satisfy what you really most need" and slides the promised Jackson note to her and says "Goodbye".

Not long after, he does purchase that mountain property he is looking for via the realtor contact information provided in the dark strip-tease joint. Then many days later he gets an impromptu call from the same realtor and she asks if he is willing to go out on a dual date with her, her husband and that same striptease woman.

Who knows why men make mistakes the way they often do? Yet, in this case, is a mistake being made, as he agrees to go on the dual date? In short, he dates that woman three times and decides that her path and his are not well enough aligned to ever justify a relationship and simply stops calling her. However six months later she calls him, crying "I have just been evicted, don't have any money and don't know what to do", "Would you be willing to let my daughter and I use one of your spare bedrooms until I get things figured out?" A silence follows as his thoughts worm their way through weeds.

"Hello ...?" She asks "Are you there?"

In fact Aspot is renting a large house with two totally empty bedrooms so offering help could cost little more than a possible messy relationship. "Tell you what" "You can find a roof here as long as you realize that I like peace in my life. I am not looking for a relationship with you.

That you strongly consider pursuing your nursing career and you do not bring any strange men into my home".

Daughter and mother quickly move in a manner which shows an intended stance of permanence but personal distance. No relationship develops, and in fact they seldom see one another for much more than a minute or two each day although he does keep an eye on her daughter while she works night hours. A couple months down the road she asks Aspot for a ride across town. He offers her a motorcycle seat behind him and follows her directions to what turns out to be a strongly guarded compound with exposed automatic firearms being held by ugly men inside the inner gate. As his bike rolls to a stop he scans the environment and whispers to her as she hops off "This is not the kind of church I was talking about". She casts him a smile and says "I won't need a ride home"

He watches as she is escorted into a large dingy looking house by a man wielding an upward pointing rifle. Silently he mutters "Whew! How sad..." kicks his bike to life, then nods at the stone faced gateman and idles out of the lifeless compound.

Not much later he notices evidence that another man (or men) is periodically sleeping in his home, raiding his refrigerator and consuming his coffee. But he leaves for work too early and she comes home too late for him to spot them. It is after his eyes get seared by the image of a naked man's butt disappearing into her room one morning that he encounters the woman that evening and reminds her that she had agreed to keep her business out of his home and gives her a deadline to either move out or find her possessions out on the front lawn with the locks changed.

Less than an hour later, Aspot hears much loud motorcycle engines and sees many riders pulling up near his front door with headlight beams piercing the front window curtain. Then what follows is an echoing, loud and definite knock on his door. Aspot calmly walks and opens the door to see a gruff tattoo faced stranger wearing much leather. Aspot scans him a moment and then asks without any quaver or fear "How may I help you?"

The stranger says "If you make my girl cry, I will cut your throat." At which the stranger does not wait for a reply but returns to his bike which is sitting atop the sidewalk directly in front of the door. Then in the company of smoke, noise, similar looking henchman, a horde of demons disappears into the dark of a night, yet still young enough, to bear much trouble.

Behind, Aspot, the woman stands watching and as he turns towards her, she drops her eyes and quietly slips into her bedroom. He can actually understand the dilemma she has built around herself and daughter and although separated by a wall, shares a type of sadness with her. He has observed with little doubt that she truly loves her daughter in some, totally messed up life style, type of way. Aspot sighs, shakes his head grabs his jacket and starts his bike while asking guidance from Above. He truly does not feel any fear even though quite certain that getting his throat sliced is not an idle threat.

He pulls out onto the highway and soon hears the Spirit whisper "Go home or you will find trouble." This makes him laugh, "What do you mean?" which is really more of a statement than a question. "Haven't I already found enough trouble for the day?" He hears again "Go back home."

Aspot does not go home but instead drops into a local bar, which is mostly empty. He orders a beer from an idle bartender who, upon finding a customer, starts a casual chat. However, he is not interested in her bar chatter and his ignore makes him more of 'a bore' than the bartender can accept, so she confronts him and says, "Whoa" "You seem to have a real heavy over you."

He looks up and says "Yep". She plants her elbows on the countertop and proceeds to weasel this evening's encounter with the motorcycle gang out of him. At one point she suddenly stands straight with concern and says "Oh no, that gang is definitely not one you want to mingle with!", "They are well known for causing people to disappear.", "Here I need to practice a new drink so will make you one. Tell me the whole story and let me know how this drink tastes" Aspot begins to report the whole story as she slides a glass into his hand and goes back to her elbows across the counter from him.

The concoction in the glass goes down easily with little taste of alcohol. Seeing that he has finished that drink she asks how he liked it, then hearing his positive reply says "Here try this one" and he receives a different elixir which again is tasty. He continues to portray the story but quickly notices that alcohol is hitting his blood stream and asks "What is in those drinks?" "Oh, they were both a mix of three pure shots" "Here let me make you make you a different one" "Oh, no! I am beginning to feel the alcohol and had better get home"

"Ok, take care!"

Almost immediately, a patrolman pulls him over for excess acceleration, books him for DUI and he loses his driver's license on the spot. So for three months he gets to work by bus, which is where, he discovers that his public transportation commute is providing the time he was promised, by God, for reading more of His Word. Yes this situation might be seen as a type of partnership in effort, but nonetheless the promise did come true.

However it also seems three months is insufficient for the duration of the promise, because after the three month period of revocation is over, he unwisely rides his motorcycle to the nearby city where he expects to get to court and get permission to re-obtain his driver's license. Heads-up: The initial suspension period was fully over, but until a revoked driver's license is appropriately re-obtained the driver's license remains, fully suspended. But, of this Aspot is confidently ignorant and feels certain that he can safely ride the relatively short distance to the courthouse. Again, hint; there is very little that is certain in this world!

As it so happens, within a block of the courthouse, another driver, coming from a side alley, does not see Aspot or his motorcycle and that driver speeds quickly out directly towards Aspot who does not notice the car until the bumper is about to crush his leg, at which time Aspot in a last instant jumps clear and lands on the car hood while his motorcycle is pushed sideways across the street by mass and motion. BTW; for the beginner, this is life and life provides 'the necessary heat for our time in the forge'.

Aspot is not hurt but very soon discovers that his antic of driving with a suspended driver's license has just bought him an additional year of Holy Scripture reading time! Looking back Aspot has said numerous times "That DUI is the best thing that could have happened to me". This is because he does read the bible while riding the bus to/from work, which literally takes three hours every day. Furthermore he has found an unexpected type of freedom by how he does not always need to spend his time driving in rush hour traffic. There are numerous ways of getting around without driving. For instance, it is great fun to ride the 'Ski Train' right to the door of a ski resort and often goes skiing with his son this way. But perhaps most important of all, is that during this season he meets God in a very personal and great faith building manner which you are about to read about.

Oh first lets close this chapter which asks a few details being explained. First within a couple of days of the initial loss of a driver's license Aspot had already bought a townhome near a bus stop and moved. He continued to pay his lease on house where the wayward mother and daughter still live. However she calls him many months later to thank him and let him know that she has partnered up with a good, safe man. That they have leased that same house and that she is back in school to become a nurse. May God continue to bless her and family!

BTW: Yes, Love does work in mysterious ways. "For the believer all things are allowed, but not everything is beneficial" In all cases being inoculated with a good dose of Love in our heart is probably the first and best defense. Yet Aspot sincerely suggests that, strongly avoiding the two dollar beers in a strip joint is one reasonable form of defense against 'the enemy' which exists only to seek and destroy.

2

INTO THE FORGE

Tidy Task

Daily now Aspot takes the bus to work which requires three bus changes both morning and night. One bus exchange in the morning requires a lengthy, 30 minute wait, where there is a sizeable lawn of a small street corner park. He quickly becomes accustomed to sitting on the bench and quietly reading until the next bus shows up.

This block corner seems to be a well maintained mini-park with the exception of much trash caught inside a large back perimeter hedge of tall bushes. Much of this hedge locked trash looks to have been neglected for many years and includes an amount of discarded small car parts which suggests that this corner had long ago been the location of an auto shop.

He decides that in addition to reading, he will spend part of each day cleaning up that hedge, and begins by first searching around the bushes for some type of container to collect trash into, with plans to then to discard it into a conveniently positioned park trashcan. He expects to find common plastic grocery bags caught within the bushes but does not find one or any other container worthy of collecting trash. Therefore he plans the following day to recycle, by bringing a plastic grocery bag from his home.

However, the following morning he is already on the first bus when he realizes he has forgotten to bring a grocery bag. So with a grunt makes a mental note to remember stuffing one into a jacket pocket when he gets home in the evening. However, he is reading the Gospel of Mathew which speaks of a man with faith strong enough to move mountains. As he reads this verse he is moved to sit back and reflect upon what kind of faith that must be...

As he continues to do so is then moved by the Spirit to ask that a bag be provided for him this morning for the purpose of accomplishing his planned task. In fact the Spirit takes a steadfast hold of his attention and he is moved to continue focusing upon only the certainly of a positive outcome from this prayer. Yes he is holding this thought and prayer very tightly... holding... holding...

Still holding this verse and, his prayer and fully expecting his prayer be answered, he exits the bus and crosses the street towards the mini-park with no thought other than finding a bag or other container. As he steps onto the street corner sidewalk he looks up and sees not one container but rather two. Two common grocery bags are in direct sight, both hanging close to each other, midway upon on the centermost bush and looking is it they had been intentionally placed this way. He approaches these bags, bows his head and says "Thank you". Then he begins his task, quickly fills both, then walks and discards them in a trash can.

Without doubt he believes these two grocery bags are a gift of provision. So thanking God again but not wanting to be a wearisome bother to Heaven he still intends to bring a bag himself the following day. However again the following morning he forgets to bring a grocery bag until after already on the bus. And even while realizing his omission he is emboldened by the Spirit and senses being told to expect a bag again waiting him. So now with perhaps beginners faith he arrives at that corner and finds the expected plastic grocery bag laying smack dab in the middle of the lawn. Bowing his head he again offers thanks to Heaven.

The next day, while getting dressed, he feels being told not to bring a bag but to expect and find one in the same spot. True to promise he finds another one lying in the middle of the lawn and offers a thank you to Heaven. Daily bags are provided and he continues to clean the hedge. The task has now taken over a month and his faith is waxing very strong.

The area around, under and between the individual stems within the large array of bushes is slowly becoming clean and one day he spots an old grocery bag caught deep inside the base and looking up speaks to Heaven, saying "You need not provide a bag tomorrow because I have found one for tomorrow" There is no surprise the following morning. As expected, God does not provide a grocery bag and he uses the old one he knows to be in the bushes. And then, again no surprise when again the following day, he does expect and finds a grocery bag provided and laying on the same spot in the middle of the lawn.

A few days later he sees another old grocery bag lying deep within the bushes and so he immediately looks upwards, to God and makes it known that he has found a bag for the following day. However when he arrives the following morning he is surprised when he finds a new grocery bag provided and laying in middle of the lawn. He quickly shrugs off wavering uncertainty to consider that God must want him to fill two bags this day, but when he attempts to retrieve the old one from the bushes he discovers the old grocery bag literally falls into many pieces and therefore is totally unusable. He is deeply moved by this lesson which speaks to him about how God always knows far better than we do about what we really need.

This mini-park cleanup effort takes a little over a month. The day came when he could only find enough trash to but partially fill the bag provided and so he knew this task to be complete. He bows his head and says "Lord I am finished cleaning this park.", "Thank you. Thank you. Thank you".

Aspot continues to ride the bus and wait at that mini-park bus stop and never again finds another grocery bag on its lawn or in its bushes. Yes he often found various new pieces of litter which he could gather in one hand and discard but it is obvious to him and now fully validated that indeed God had actively participated in the mini-park clean up task by daily providing him the needed cleanup grocery bags. This is a gift of much faith, which Aspot remains eternally thankful. And if you are willing to allow him to consider such a grand thought, for those days of the task, it was, for him, a type of literal walk with God.

Eventually, however, Aspot begins to notice bicyclists who with backpacks appear to be commuting. Before we continue let us take a moment and ask God to bless everyone who appreciates the, often volunteer, effort it takes to well maintain parks, sidewalks, roads and the environment in which we all live. Also let us ask God to bless those who help preserve some of the natural oil resources for our grandchildren by using public, shared or an alternate type of transportation when possible.

Three rings

When a boy Aspot never owned or had access to a useable bicycle. This is simply because he grew up on a remote farm where it was generally either by horse, truck or tractor that he was riding. Well that is until the day his dad showed up with two brand new, full sized, of modest engine displacement dirt bikes which, with great joy, immediately replaced the horse for cattle herding. But we are talking about bicycles which he has rarely been on and what this means is that his now thirties-something leg muscles have never been developed in the manner needed to pedal a bicycle many miles.

Therefore it is with reasonable trepidation that he purchases a bicycle with hope of commuting the distance between his home and place of work which is, as the crow flies, about twelve miles each direction. The task seems daunting and his first attempt is made on a weekend morning where failure would not cause being late for work. Nonetheless he sets his mind and with surprise finds the twelve miles is not as bad as anticipated. So the following Monday he makes his first bicycle commute to work. Over time his leg strength develops and the bicycle commute becomes a daily source of enjoyment rather than an arduous ordeal.

Now remember his driver's license is yet suspended, which is actually the real reason he is choosing to bicycle commute. And yes, this does eliminate the time provided him to read scripture, but he is now actually finding time to read at home because the Word has somehow become more important than many other distractions, such as watching television. Besides now, while commuting, his mind and attention is not focused upon the road, other cars or the commute but simply upon the moments of a peaceful and Spirit filled bicycle ride.

Although the route he takes does run alongside some streets, it in general, hits the many Denver bicycle paths and through Cherry Creek Park. So his attention in mind and heart is for singing and talking with God. At least once daily he is found reciting a rather long traditional prayer sequence which his family has daily recited before bed throughout his youth on that farm and even to this day. So when he visits his parents, he remains eager to join their daily recital of this same prayer sequence. Some call this type of prayer "rote" but it is not puffed up and he believes it to be a powerful prayer. At this time, in life, he is often spotted singing, praying and talking with God as he pedals the miles of bicycle paths and lanes with little thought of anything but Life.

Nevertheless, he is also looking forward to the day he gets his driver's license back and can also ride that two wheeled vehicle called a motorcycle. ☺ With this anticipation in mind he starts to replace his motorcycle, which had been destroyed near the courthouse, by preparing to build one in the middle of his living room. Yes, true to rumor, fanatics do build motorbikes in their living rooms. This new bike is primarily arriving by parcel carriers as he orders hundreds of individual motorcycle parts. He is willing to pay the extra cost associated with the promise that the chosen part is made in the USA. But then he considers himself to be an "Always love your country, but never trust your government" kind of man.

Because he had grown up using a fully equipped shop on the family farm which employed metal lathes and milling tools, in his youth had developed the basic metal machining knowledge and so he augments the tools he used for his motorcycle project with a used but decent, engine lathe and a combination horizontal and vertical milling machine which he installs in his townhome car garage.

However he also soon becomes troubled in heart when reading the book of Genesis and notices that the 'sons of Cain' are described as being metal-smiths and immediately feels conviction. So he asks, "Does this mean that working with metal is contrary to your will Lord?" and immediately stops using the metal working equipment to wait for guidance.

For a week he prays this way but when making a needed bicycle repair receives an explicit answer as follows; He maintains various nuts and bolts in small plastic bags as counted from bulk bins within a local hardware store. He searches for and finds one such bag that he knows to contain only lock-washers, of the size needed. These lock-washers he had only recently, obtained at the hardware store where they were priced for so-many cents each. At that time had individually counted them from the store bin into a bag for purchase. What is being declared is that Aspot had visually observed each lock-washer individually because he had manually counted them and knows the condition of each.

But now, reaching blindly into this bag, his fingers pinching a washer, draws it from the bag. However, it comes out of the bag, not alone as expected, but rather with two more. These washers are not just stuck together but rather physically interlocked like a chain. "Wow!" he exclaims, "This is really quite odd". And then he quietly examines and ponders how they could have become interlocked in such a manner. He examines the remainder of the washers and verifies that they are all yet individual. He has never before seen any lock-washers find a way to engage themselves together this way before. And although each has a slit, a part of the locking mechanism, it is so tight that it would take exact alignment of slits and much force to pressure together even two washers in this fashion. In fact for even two of these washers to engage in this fashion, on their own, is virtually impossible. Furthermore it was not just two washers linked together but three! The odds of this string of washers becoming interlocked, by chance on their own can only be against astronomically staggering odds.

The following weekend Aspot took the bus and retrieved his son just he did every other weekend. When his son, now sixteen, heard the story he became determined to prove, to his dad, that it was just by chance they had become linked. So his son took this string of washers out to the garage where using two pairs pliers worked hard to slide any two apart. After failing to get any of them even to start sliding apart he grabs two pairs of vice-grip style pliers. Indeed, after more than thirty minutes of much squeezing, wiggling, pulling, tugging effort he does eventually manage to worm two of the washers apart but then humbly later tells his dad the story and admits that he now believes it was impossible for even two of these washers to have ever slid together on their own.

Aspot believes this chain of three lock-washers was woven by God to show him it is OK to work metal. Nevertheless he also believes that God asks him to keep Him (the Father, Son and Holy Spirit), in mind while metal-working. This same rule, Aspot now considers, equally important for all types of quality work. May God bless your hands and mind as you work, with Him in heart.

Shields Up!

One of the best benefits of getting older is the fact that all of the numerous experiences in our lives offer tricks about how to perform a task perhaps easier or faster or better and generally with greater quality. In fact, it seems that good work generally requires some amount of artistic finesse within the methods employed to accomplish it, regardless of what type the work might be. A quality product requires careful attention which might also come only after some well-honed skill possibly only obtained from years of continued mindful practice.

Excellence, if not perfection, can be said to be a type of virtue that employs both the use of our hands and head with heartfelt inner strength and precision. Good work on a repeatable basis can only be achieved when we purpose our goal to include an acceptable measure of virtue. This line of thought about quality is only being mentioned for the purpose of setting anchors into bedrock. Let us firmly take hold of the fact that nothing 'substantial and good' is ever accomplished by meager lackluster effort or without some amount of help from Heaven.

Our Lord expressly tells us "All good comes from Heaven". This is an important truth to keep in at the forefront of all work, when we truly wish to see 'good' results come from our efforts. Quality of anything includes some amount of polishing only obtained from virtue provided in part from Heaven. Aspot fully believes this to be a fundamental truth of no small importance. We can all be certain that if 'any good' be found on these pages then the 'good' is only from Heaven.

This very thought is on the forefront of Aspot's mind one day as he is working on his motorcycle and is moved to examine the environment within which he is working. He looks around with no surprise acknowledges his certainty that the environment is comfortable and reasonably clean. But then he feels further moved as if there is some form of discomfort in the room. He hears, in heart, "Is this song you are now listening appropriate?" Aspot responds "What do you mean by appropriate?" The Holy Spirit replies "Appropriate for me".

Aspot likes music, yet picky about the melody and how well the musicians play their instruments, but with little attention to the song lyrics. However he now feels prompted to listen to the words being sung and immediately feels ashamed by what he hears being broadcast from the speakers. Without any further guidance he immediately removes that CD from his player and discards it into a trashcan looks up and says "Thank you" then goes back to work on the emerging motorcycle.

Across many following days his music inventory changes dramatically as he listens carefully to every CD as it plays. When hearing any song that feels being possibly offensive to the Holy Spirit that CD is immediately discarded. Eventually approximately only one half of his music collection remains. What Aspot has done is pay respect to God and asked for His greater presence and thereby also His help.

Yes, his music collection has radically diminished but soon, he happens into a nearby Christian book and music store and begins to appreciate a music genre he has never previously considered and finds with much amazement the quality of most of the selections he chose to listen to while in the music store. In fact he determines that the Christian music genre, in general is, quite often, most excellent in every manner. So his CD carrousel player slowly becomes again almost filled with a good selection of both secular and Christian selections which seem acceptable to the Holy Spirit and the spirit of his home work place.

Construction of his motorcycle continues in a casual spare time basis. Parts needing any milling or painting get attention in the garage while assembly is comfortably and peacefully performed inside his townhome. Meanwhile, in his garage is now also an ongoing restoration of a 1960 VW beetle, a fixer-upper, Aspot has purchased for his son as a father/son project. So every other weekend this bug is getting attention by son and father together. One of these weekends the two are discussing paint schemes for both the VW and the emerging motorcycle.

The general color scheme for Aspot's motorcycle has already been decided and many of the parts, including the frame and engine, have already been painted. Yet he is not yet satisfied with possible designs for the artwork design to go on the tanks and fenders. When his son hears about his dad's paint scheme dilemma, he says "You know dad, we recently studied the Roman army general named Constantine and he had all of his soldiers paint crosses on their shields and history shows that his army since that time never lost any further battles despite at times against staggering odds" "I personally think it was only just luck, but you might want to consider painting a cross on your tanks because I have often seen random bruises on your other bikes and know you can use all the extra amount of help you can get!"

Aspot smiles at his son with much love because it is a great idea and because it shows some amount of cracking in the hard enamel of his son's skin in regards to properly considering God. Let's dwell on this thought for a moment. You see both by the sheer apathy of his son's mother and by what his son has told him, one or more school counselors have literally deeply engrained into him the thought that God and the bible are nothing but fantasy stories for weak minded people. At the time he had discovered that his son thought such things Aspot had tried to offer counter thinking, but his son's ears were closed and the endgame of that discussion had resulted in rather loud verbal contention. This was an incident which Aspot now tries to avoid although he yet insists that his son attend church, with him, the weekends they are together.

Anyway the cross for protection concept is a good one and Aspot now desires to employ it. Various versions of the cross concept are tried but all themes are in a rather concealed cross fashion so that he need not much worry about offending any of his biker companions. Nothing he tries seems adequate until finally he was moved by the Holy Spirit and hears "Aspot, get serious, if you want me to protect you then do not be ashamed of either me or The Cross."

This move of spirit cuts Aspot to the core and causes him to blush. First of all, God has often shown Aspot what love means and because of this Aspot is falling deeply in love with God. Therefore he truly wishes to likewise show love and please the Lord. Furthermore, during many years of motorcycle riding experience he has often encountered automobile situations and very well aware how seemingly invisible smaller vehicles can be to other drivers.

In fact, a year before where the story in this book started he encountered an extremely bad motorcycle accident when an automobile driver illegally turning around by using an interstate utility vehicle median crossing pulled out directly in front of Aspot, causing a broadside car impact at about seventy five miles an hour. Yet that accident of itself is not what is important. Rather of importance is that accident had caused a brief out-of-body, out-of-this-world, visit with God. Let it be said, that no miracle seen in this world, will ever change anyone quite as distinctly as even the briefest visit with God in the other world.

By all means, protection provided by God is greatly desired, so following the divine rebuke, he paints big bold crosses as a blatant focal point of the design and with emphasis brightly emblazoned on the front corners of the tanks. Now with the tank and other body parts finished in pearled paints and multiple layers of clear-coat so that as the individual body parts are carried from the garage to the living room they sparkle brilliantly in the bright morning sunshine.

Soon the last bit of assembly is peacefully accomplished as he tightens the last screw. Now the bike is completed, polished, handsome, certainly eye candy and potentially worth a small fortune. On the one hand this is pleasing but then on the other is an issue of concern and this is the fact that this motorcycle is not yet titled anywhere to anyone and so there is no way to prove it belongs to him should anyone take hold of it.

Although the frame has a vehicle identification number stamped upon it, this machine in not registered in his name until this frame and motorcycle are examined at a Department of Transportation. This means that any thief could steal this bike and get it easily titled in their name without any bit of a problem. Since he has no proof of ownership this motorcycle is at great risk should a thief see it sitting in his garage. This is an uncomfortable situation which he cannot remedy until he can get it to the Department of Transportation and this first requires him to first re-obtain a driver's license which is still months ahead.

Therefore every morning/evening as he retrieves/returns his commuting bicycle, from the garage, he always watches the garage door go down to make sure make sure it goes firmly closed. However, one morning, after watching the garage door fully close and after having returned the garage door remote to its location on the kitchen counter, when he begins the bicycle route to work, in the spirit, he hears "Check your garage door". This notion he shrugs off because he has just visually verified that the garage door went fully closed. So he continues to pedal towards work. It always takes a bit of pedaling to get warmed up and into the groove of the bicycle commute and so the first couple of minutes are extra effort anyway because the first quarter of a mile is up a relatively steep hill.

This morning as he slowly climbs that hill he again hears a whisper that suggests him to believe that his garage door is sitting open. But in his mind this is still a nonsense worry. Yet the thought continues to outright nag him and the farther he rides the louder this thought becomes until his spirit is yelling "Your garage door is open". At which he now actually verbally replies "No, I am certain it is closed!"

Finally the nagging voice in his head wins and he turns around, rides some miles back home feeling certain that he is just being a stupid worry-wart. He intends to only quickly circle past his garage and then speedily pedal back up that hill. But as he clears the corner of his home he can see his motorcycle fully exposed, brightly shining in the sunshine, saying "Please take me". Aspot feels a strong blood rush and rising of neck hair! His garage door is indeed fully wide open.

After carefully inspecting the garage doorway he finds nothing out of the ordinary. So he walks around the corner of his home to the front door and retrieves the garage door remote. Coming back around the corner, using the remote he watches the garage door go fully closed and stay closed. So he walks back around the corner and leaves the remote laying on the counter in his home and returns to his bicycle in front of the garage but once again finds that the garage door unexpectedly wide open.

It does not take long before he discovers that, every time he lays the remote, for the garage door, back down upon his kitchen counter the garage door goes back open. This he also soon finds is caused by an internal metal switch lever having become loose and shorting a circuit board in just the right fashion to cause the door to go open as he lays it down. He quickly and permanently fixes this problem. Since that day he has never again felt tugged to double check the garage door nor has he ever again found that garage door unexpectedly open.

Because of the manner in which he had been moved to hear and obey that voice in his head he attributes this to a lesson of Holy Spirit voice discernment and to the care of God concerning those Crosses brightly painted on the front corners of his motorcycle gas tanks. In any case this incident is yet another gift of increasing faith.

By the way, it has been many years since that morning. He still rides the same motorcycle. He has never encountered even one mishap or accident on it and by faith, has remained absolutely positive that both he and his bike's protection are being actively covered by God. Let us pray "Thank you God for how you bless us", "Help us daily Lord to find the strength, knowledge and willingness to bless you."

Where the Wind Goes

It is now a warm sunny day, Aspot and a good friend sit at an outside patio table discussing events of the day.

These friends often meet for various reasons including a weekly bible study. But not today, it is hot and they are just relaxing, slathered with sunscreen, sporting only shorts and lazily soaking up the warmth of the brightly radiating sun and the peace of the day. The sky is clear and the atmosphere breathless, without any hint of wind. It is casual conversation with no agenda while they perspire and slowly sip a beer from their quickly warming once ice cold bottles.

Yet it does not take long to invite God to join into their discussion by the way they begin to ruminate the manner in which the Holy Spirit seems to be moving their lives. Perhaps it is because the atmosphere is chokingly muggy without a hint of even the slightest zephyr that they begin to speak of the 'Wind'. Aspot's friend opens his bible and begins to read aloud "The wind blows where it wishes and you hear its sound, but cannot tell where it comes from, and where it goes. So is everyone who is born of the Spirit."

At exactly the moment this verse is finished by reading "the Spirit" the atmosphere is suddenly a livened by an exceedingly strong wind. The eyes of both men are widened as a gale of great force immediately lifts empty lawn chairs into the air and spreads them widely. Garbage cans complain with loud racket as they are quickly toppled and their lids carried speedily across the patio to bang against a shed clear across the lawn! Tall elm trees are bent and held far to one side so that they audibly groan from the strain, with many leaves and small limbs stripped and carried away! This wind continues fiercely, for roughly a minute, but then as suddenly as this wind had started it simply ceases entirely … not even a whimper of a breeze remains but rather only a deep, heavy … restless calm.

Although the atmosphere is again become very still and silent the two men's hearts are left racing with a feeling of having been hit by a small strike of lightening. They exchange a meaningful wide eyed glance and without saying a word share a silent, profound spiritual discussion. The coals are being wafted, Carbon is migrating into pores and crud is being burned away as the Craftsman, softly, silently and effectively works.

Tracking the Holy Spirit

Half an hour later these two men are still sitting quietly and pondering when two teenagers wander into the yard and offer to sell magazines. This is the friend's home whom is a very personable man and who quickly turns their dialogue around to discover a little bit about them.

At first, Aspot listens with little interest to their discussion which is mainly aimed at selling magazines but senses a wistful demeanor of spirit trying to speak from one of these teenage boys. It does not surprise him when one of the teenagers begins to vocalize an interest in the bibles he sees laying on the patio table. At this time Aspot joins the discussion which becomes briefly centered on merits of studying the Word.

As the teenagers prepare to exit by gathering their materials back into their backpacks, Aspot suggests "If you should ever want to talk further about the Word, give one of us a call". The one young man looks at him silently for a moment, then walks back and asks for a phone number. Aspot writes phone numbers upon a piece of note paper and hands it back, not really ever expecting to hear from either of them.

However about three months later, to his surprise, that one young man calls "Hello, you probably don't remember me, but I met you when selling magazines earlier this year and you gave me your phone numbers.".," Well we are back in town and I", pause "I need help."

Perhaps the wind that day had kicked dust which had settled upon this young man's shoulders? In any case it is quickly understood that this man is simply at a crossroads, with a desire in his heart to find Life. However he feels trapped in a suitcase situation, with little chance of breaking free because he does not know how. This is largely because he receives little more than food and a bed while selling magazines, which means him and others he travels with, are possibly being grossly misused, trapped and purposefully left too uneducated to develop a reasonable life plan for how to get permanently off the bus.

This young man is from a distinctly broken family of which most contact is lost and with little hope of seeing help come from anyone he knows. So now he is talking to Aspot with hope that he can, find any guidance, a safe exit from an empty journey, almost begging, with a sincere plea for help. With few words, this young man, has revealed that his childhood learning capacity has been squandered by teaching him little more than to disdain, the dog eat dog mentality, of the inner city, from which he originally came.

Being moved to help, Aspot agrees to meet with him the following Sunday afternoon in a public setting, beside the pool of the motel where his group is currently staying, at a specific time. Come Sunday morning, Aspot arrives at church early to pray, in particular, about the young man, how to guide him and what he expects the meeting with him might reveal. As he prays he hears the Holy Spirit whisper, "Take someone with you." Aspot is moved to believe this is good advice, not because of danger, but rather so that the young man can know that everyone is held accountable, by a third party, for whatever decision the meeting might bring. Believing that this is true guidance, Aspot is confident he will bump into someone willing to help during church fellowship which always follows the morning service.

The church begins to fill and a young woman, he knows to be the daughter of one of the pastors takes a seat beside him and offers a quick smile. Aspot had met her a few months earlier when she first returned home from a missionary journey. She had, at that time, hinted an interest in getting a short ride on his motorcycle. Although he had discounted that mention as being a polite hello pleasantry her request did come back to mind as a possible blessing this day.

When the Sunday service ends Aspot asks if she is still interested in the short motorcycle ride. She responds "Yes". So he then continues to share with her the real reason he is offering her a ride, which is to be that 'someone' to take along to meet with the teenager. After revealing his motive for offering her a ride he again asks if she is still interested at which she replies "Oh, most certainly".

The afternoon turns out to be truly lovely, starting with a lunch and getting to know a little bit more about one another. Later, on schedule, they ride to the motel and together walk towards the pool where the young man is waiting. It is determined that he just needs a place to stay, long enough to get a real job and earn enough money to get a place of his own. Aspot agrees to feed, house and provide other necessities for him during the interim. We can quickly summarize the young man's journey by saying that he does quickly find a job, saves money and within a few months moves out to live on his own.

In the meantime the young woman and Aspot continue to meet at church and soon at the same evening bible study being held at his friend's home. Although she is quite lovely and exhibits a delightful personality she is also more than ten years younger than Aspot and so he does not entertain any notion of relationship beyond pure friendship with her.

Besides he already knows this woman to be a daughter of one of the pastors at the same church and inherently regards her as being part of a far holier train than his. However, he notices that she is not shy in showing attraction to him and so he expresses, to her, reason to carefully avoid any relationship beyond being just good friends. Nevertheless, attraction still continues even though now more subtly in an unspoken mutually acceptable and pleasing fashion.

3

BREATHING CARBON

L ife, in general, also continues to develop. The
Volkswagen beetle, belonging to his son, is still in
his garage but nearing completion of both inside and
outside restoration. Aspot continues to bicycle commute
daily during all seasons to work but does spend recreational
time with his son in the Colorado Rocky Mountains and
takes off three weeks to build a modest shed style cabin in
the Black Hills of South Dakota upon an isolated piece
of property, near the edge of a limestone outcropping,
above a gurgling brook. At that time he also purchases
two modestly powered, full size, dirt trail motorcycles and
so father and son explore many local logging roads and
discover abandoned mine structures. It is a fun, exciting
and pleasant period of his Life.

The coal bed is beginning to glow as wind now silently,
slowly and purposefully moves. Back home in Colorado
he is asleep in the middle of the night and enters another
dream that starts with "Listen, I have something to tell you."
And although Aspot is asleep, he is also very aware that he
is asleep and dreaming in a fashion atypical to the usual.

Aspot is walking through a dense corn field with the tassels hanging far above his head. He encounters an old abandoned pickup truck and using it as a ladder climbs first into the bed and then on top its cab to see across the top of field. The field seems to stretch endlessly in all directions about him.

"What do you think?" A previously unnoticed old man with a white beard, leaning against the wooden truck sideboards asks and startles Aspot. Aspot scans this man and knows he is from Heaven then responds "Well, I do not know. What are you asking?" The old man smiles and nodding his head to show direction says "Look over there what do you see?" Aspot turns his head and at first sees only the corn stalk tassels. "I see only this corn field" The old man says "Look a bit harder" Aspot looks that direction again and this time clearly sees the steeple of a white clapboard church little different from the one, when young, his family used to attend that stood atop a river break bluff. "Oh, I see a church", "Why do you ask?"

"Here lets go take a look at it" Immediately Aspot and the old man were standing alongside a modest sized, white clapboard church with a cross bearing steeple, of a style once common in rural America. Aspot steps back against the corn to get a better look and immediately notices the windows are boarded closed, in a crisscross fashion that showed that whoever had done the boarding was neither caring about either weather elements or vandals getting in but rather simply making the statement "This church is out of service".

Aspot and the Old Man walked around the outside of this building and notes that it is still in a recently well maintained condition even though all openings are boarded and well hidden amongst much corn in the

39

middle of a field. The old man looking keenly at Aspot again asks "What do you think?" Aspot considers the corn all about them and understands and feels the same impression The Lord made two thousand years ago and responds "I feel sad".

Suddenly the Old Man and Aspot still walking are upon a very wide, well maintained golf course which abruptly ends against rocky cliff dropping towards an ocean that show waves lapping against a sidewise rock base in the distance. In the other direction looms a tall wooden skeleton of a large building that looks as though long ago it had been started being built but never finished. They walk to this skeleton and climb stairs and step onto a large solid feeling floor which looks to be complete and appealing aside from possibly needing years of oxidation being polished off it. Over their heads loomed pillars to which sidewall posts and bare rafters are attached.

Scattered across the floor are stacks of building materials that look to have been left uncared for possibly a bit too long and show signs of severe weather deterioration and visible rot. One more time the Old Man asks "What do you think?" Aspot, is not yet sure what he is being shown but in conjunction with the previous vision has a good inkling, says "The foundation of this building seems very firm and solid but something needs to be done to finish it before what was started becomes totally ruined.", "It looks as though someone has been putting more effort into the golf course than this building"

The Old Man sighs and nods his head "Yes", "This is My Church.", "Watch this" at which the Old Man turn towards the green lawn and Aspot begins to see the golf ball holes in the lawn, each with a distinctive "Pop" disappear so that nothing but a dark green lawn surrounds the structure. Aspot observes sadness in face of the Old Man who seems, perhaps a bit, uneasy about being too closely analyzed and looks towards the lawn to say "A plain lawn is just much nicer", "Here I have something for you" and leads Aspot to a small room at one end of the structure where He brushes off dust from a cabinet that appears to be a type of safe for valuables. Then He opens its door and pulls out a small object, which Aspot recognizes, and hands it to Aspot. "Take care of this until I return"

Now they suddenly stand at the brink of a precipice above what looks like a meteor crater but with a small hill that has a green leafed tree standing near the center. The crater is open at one end and through this gap could again be seen the ocean shining in the distance. The Old Man waves his hand over the crater and water begins to flow from the base of the small center hill out towards the ocean.

The Old Man is looking intently at Aspot and says, "Now prepare and wait" then the Old Man disappears leaving Aspot standing alone at the craters edge. In his hand he is tightly holding the object entrusted to him, pondering everything he has been shown and what the terrain now seen by the light of a setting sun might mean.

Life continues, and Aspot feels the Spirit moving and is reaching for heaven as hard as he knows how.

Ten Pennies

A much later Sunday morning, following church, that same delightful woman and Aspot decide to walk for lunch together through the warm sunshine. Shortly he reaches to retrieve a dime from the sidewalk. "Yippee!" he exclaims and tells her that he regards even pennies, found on pavement, as being worthy acceptable gifts from God. Yes, in his mind, even a penny has value to a humble heart. "When enough have been found, you can buy a mansion." All good things come from God and therefore denying small gifts might be cause for also missing the larger ones.

Aspot continues speaking "Generally I find only pennies, but I have noticed that whenever you are with me I am being blessed and find dimes". In fact he had picked up two dimes, that afternoon, they had both responded, to a call for help from a stranger. He casts a smile towards her and she having felt the affectionate note of his monetary discourse with a giggle brushes her shoulder against his and asks "Would you still feel blessed if you found ten pennies rather than a dime?" They both laugh at the light-hearted thought as they continue to walk through the pleasant warmth of late morning sunshine.

However, no more than about two hundred yards later as they pass through a mostly empty strip mall parking lot they both abruptly stop and look at each other because closely scattered on the tar directly ahead can be seen a number of pennies. He quickly begins to gather them while counting " …, 8, 9, 10". After scanning about but finding no more, they both feel immense joy and she reaches over and takes his hand and leans against him as they again continue to walk, even though now, a bit more silently as he ponders what this might mean?

Finding exactly ten pennies immediately following her remark seems nothing short of totally extraordinary and with a smile he squeezes her hand and absorbs the beautiful profile of her face in a more meaningful manner and her gentle signs of affection. In fact from that point on he now openly and willing proceeds to romantically court his beautiful woman friend.

Hailstone Hello

Music is unaffected by an excessively rocky road as Aspot's Jeep bounces and navigates toward a small cabin, his son helped him build years ago, in the Black Hills of South Dakota. It is a beautiful morning and his heart beats lively as he ponders the lovely woman who has recently accepted his marriage proposal.

Entering the cabin he notices much dust kick up as he drops his sleeping bag upon a table and scans to ensure rodents have not yet been able to infiltrate the cabin's modest perimeter. Then with joy of heart he goes back out into the early morning sunshine and edges out onto the limestone ledge and listens to the gentle gurgle of the brook nearly a hundred feet below. Rather dreamily he sits with legs dangling and opens his hand to release wildflower seeds into a breeze and towards the ground along the brook while a chipmunk sits on a rock ears perched and listens as he sings.

Meanwhile, on the other side of the canyon, through the tops of spruce, pine and birch trees, can be seen the steep arch roof of an Alpine style lodge building, that in the past, had been the main building of a failed Christian retreat center which Aspot, many years earlier, had been an active volunteer. The reason it had failed was largely because of the rugged condition of the same canyon bottom road, especially following every annual springtime snow melt. He has observed the narrow canyon walls channeling the deep rushing, if not raging, water and seen the multi-feet diameter culverts ripped out of the crossings and wrapped tightly around tree trunks. The hosts of the retreat center with funds exhausted and much effort finally obligingly stopped fighting Mother Nature who seems intent on keeping the road nearly impassible except for the most ardent of four-wheel rock crawlers.

But this thought he decidedly casts away because today is truly lovely and he chooses to become quiet and enjoy the song of meadowlarks and lightheartedly soaks the warmth of the environment and lounges with his feet still dangling. Oh, it feels so very good to feel loved by someone you love ...

By late morning he is now considering his reason for working his way, to this isolated location, which is to spend idle vacation time and practice handgun control. So, after gathering himself, he trots back to the cabin, grabs a package of paper shooting targets and navigates his jeep down across the creek and up, steeply, into a large open parking area of the defunct and perpetually vacant retreat center parking lot.

With a large hammer he drives a solid wooden stake deep of a sturdy target located so that shells as fired would land harmlessly into the side of a hill guarded only by silent trees. It is an absolutely perfect day for target practice, the sun is bright and no hint of wind. It is wonderful view from this high side of the canyon wall with a clear view of a huge agricultural irrigation reservoir, shimmering, in the far horizon beyond the canyon opening.

Pacing off a distance of fifty feet he fires a few rounds, from his 45 caliber handgun, and notes a wild bullet pattern. He moves closer to the target for constraining the group pattern in a fashion helpful for figuring out what he is doing wrong. Now at only thirty feet the grouping is tight about the bulls-eye and a smug sense of satisfaction causes a small smirk as he again repeatedly broadcasts additional gunfire to hear affirming echo replies from far down the canyon.

After successfully punching out the center of the target he sets his handgun down and goes to inspect the target. Kneeling on one knee he leans forward and intently examines the pattern in particular the few wild holes which are all off in the same direction which at least indicates he is making the same mistake every so often. Overall however he is really but vainly admiring his "excellent" marksmanship. "Hmm, not too shabby" he says to himself. Then eager to punch holes into a fresh target, he jumps to his feet and quickly spins back towards his jeep.

However, even before finishing one step, "WHUMPF", something heavy hits the ground directly behind him. Startled he sputters and spins back around towards the target and instantly spots, at his toes, one very large and sharply bristled hailstone!

"Ah!" with a shocked yell he darts in urgency towards the underside of his jeep for cover. But, after only three leaping steps, he calmly stops and looks up into a perfectly blue, clear, noontime sky. It is yet windless and the sun is still shining brightly. Fear of a killer hailstorm is immediately quelled and, with quaking reverence, he walks back to the target but this time to examine that hailstone. It is still lying where it landed, roughly twelve inches, directly in front of the practice target. He kneels, bows his head, closes his eyes and considers God.

For him it is intuitively obvious that God has just sent him a most certain "Hello" that speaks much more. As he examines this incredible hailstone, he observes its long bristles of ice, spiked in all directions. However, the day is hot and these spikes are rapidly melting into shorter cone shaped extrusions. The core of this hailstone is five to six inches in diameter and so if including the length of original bristles, as seen, it can be claimed to be nearly one foot in diameter. At this time it still lies exactly where the noontime shadow of his head was cast upon the ground, as he had studied the practice target, only a moment before this stunning hailstone punched the earth.

Now picking up the certain God tossed 'hello' he feels its weight, touches his tongue to taste a water drop at the end of one of the melting bristles and is filled with an awestruck marvel. Looking up he acknowledges God and again notes that no clouds can be seen anywhere in the sky. He carries the hailstone back to his jeep and now from this view he notices one small very dense and dark cloud hiding the peak of a high hill, at the edge of the mountains and plains. He guesses this isolated cloud to be the location from which God has cast this hailstone. Because that hill is isolated and a modest college based town at the base of the Black Hills lies between it and this location, he can somewhat accurately estimate this hailstone had sailed a twenty mile aimed toss from God.

Indeed the Creator's glory is proclaimed all around him and even sung, in part, by this large spired ball of ice which only minutes earlier had been fashioned by God's hand.

His jeep is without its top and so the sun continues to brush his brow as he lays the hailstone in a shadow under the dash and watches it slowly melt while he ponders what this 'Hello' might mean. There is much heat of the day but no wind, so again he picks up the hailstone, acknowledges its sturdy density and he blesses himself by running its coolness around his neck and brow. The Holy Spirit now feels strongly present! Aspot bows his head and asks "Lord, what are you trying to tell me?"

He perceives a whisper from within. "So you think you are a pretty good shot huh?" These Holy Spirited words carry a tone of humor and Aspot can feel His chuckle. But the tone becomes more serious. "Ok, now tell me how your aim compares to mine." "Consider the hailstone I sent and where I stood as I called your name." "Is your mark precisely timed?"

He considers the absolutely precise timing and aim of God. Then shudders as he realizes that if he had delayed but a fraction of a second in jumping up to continue practice he might have certainly been found later with the back of his head bashed in and quite dead. And with only his jeep and shoe tracks in the area and the ice melted, it would have been quite a mystery for some police officer! But he knows that such an incident would never have happened, regardless of his movement, because God knew exactly where Aspot was going to be at the exact instant that hailstone was going to be passing through the exact same space as his head had occupied only a short moment earlier. "By the mercy of God we learn to fear Him"

The Holy Spirit speaks further "As my aim and timing are perfect, so must you aim likewise" Aspot clearly understands this statement is NOT about firearm practice, but rather our individual roles, as provided and guided by Love (God), to 'walk it out with Him' (the key?).

Then tone of the Holy Spirit became as stern as the bristles on that hailstone, "Oh, but you do make much noise" "Are you not aware this place where you make loud racket is blessed and made holy by Me?", "Do you not have other places to make idle noise?" Aspot is well aware that on numerous occasions in the past the outdoor alter had been used during church services of various faith groups to consecrate and serve Holy Communion. As he considered this and many other ways these grounds might have been sanctified, the Holy Spirit moves and warms, in tone, within him. He feels a kiss and then the Spirit becomes silent.

After gathering his target back into his jeep Aspot apologizes to Heaven and then walks about the premises while continuing to soak in the presence of the Spirit. It was days later, while pondering the hailstone that he suddenly slaps himself on the forehead and wonders why he had not thought to rush, that day of the hailstone hello, to the distant hill sporting the dense dark cloud, to climb and search for God. Perhaps he missed the perfect Invitation? Sigh ...

Irish coffee

The lovely woman, who captured Aspot's heart, becomes his wife and he is now her husband by God approved intimacy upon a charming bed within a gracefully arrayed grandiose castle tower bedroom suite. Let it be known that the necessary formality of a traditional Christian marriage had occurred earlier this morning. Life is beautiful and it seems that the end of the universe is their limits! Yet, he is somberly reminded "Remain diligent."

"Oh, but of course" he casually replies, but then why not be exceedingly optimistic? After all, his new wife is a strong Christian woman, a top of the class graduate, the valedictorian speaker of a renowned Christian bible college. Aspot is filled with the confidence of a solid relationship with God in Heaven. They are a pair well suited for any battle. What can possibly go wrong? He wears a smile from ear to ear and within his heart a band plays loudly and perhaps proudly!?

They spend their honeymoon in Ireland which, by chance, happens during the middle of a widespread Mad Cows Disease scare that closed many of the sights, in Ireland, that they had hoped to visit. However they had time instead to greatly enjoy inspecting many old stone churches. Some of these are yet in use while others have been long abandoned with roofs missing, open walls partially tumbled and overgrown with green vines, often sporting grave headstones set by pious locals within the confines of half tumbled stone church walls and foliage now covering ancient church floors. Some of these old churches, of which there were many, were only found by close observation because they are almost entirely hidden amongst dense foliage. Both Aspot and wife search for headstones of possible ancestors but find only two graves bearing the last names they are looking for.

BTW; it is proven that the best Irish coffee, is indeed, truly found only in the local back road cafes.

Stone fences...

Trouble is brewing ... Aspot can feel it's very subtle form, but refuses to acknowledge it. Besides they are traveling a delightfully wandering back road of this lovely Irish landscape north towards another bed and breakfast room already waiting for them. A local map depicts a roadside trailhead stop approaching and they have high hopes of enjoying a hike through an old Irish forest. However, they wonder as they observe millions of aging tree stumps, for miles, of a forest that had either been harvested or possibly just cleared following a large fire without any intent to leave seedling trees or replant it. When they pass a recently badly burned car, they feel sorrow for the poor fellow whose car, they assume, must have been destroyed by an engine fire.

Now, at last, they can see tall trees looming, which is about where the map seems to indicate the trailhead can be found anyway. As they turn a bend they spot the trail head but are overcome immediately with shock and amazement as they choke on the smoke of another car, yet still burning. It had apparently just been left by unsuspecting hikers, at the same trail head of which they were themselves seeking. Aspot turns towards his wife and says "I do not think that we want to explore this trail after all." He senses the very present lingering spirit of contention between 'the green' and 'the orange'. It seems that this area is actually a very real 'no man's land' a type of fence between brothers.

As they speed away, Aspot struggles a surreal feeling with a hint of vertigo as he unwillingly ponders the day before when another fire, if not the same one, had started, shortly after arising from sleep. His new wife had, at that time, said "Your entire family is Catholic and are going to burn in Hell unless you do something to help save them". This was a rather unexpected outcry the third day of their honeymoon and Aspot was taken aback, not sure what to do with what his new wife had just said. Hoping it would be beneficial he tried to offer a reasonable intermediary reply "Wait a minute, do you really think God is carelessly allowing many hundreds of millions of people to perish simply because they hold a different view of Him and Life than we do?"

Aspot must have spoken more assertively than he intended because she immediately began to cry. Meanwhile Aspot had suddenly, feeling extremely awkward, became immediately quiet to watch and wonder why his new wife found reason to profusely sob. After many minutes of utter bewilderment, he had silently left their room to take a very troubled, lonely walk through an otherwise sweet green Irish meadow.

Sigh ... purpose ...?

Back home they quickly sell the townhome, which is too small and at the suggestion of the musician friend rent a cottage, delightfully located on a large piece of rather agricultural property amidst the otherwise busy shuffle of Denver suburbs. Life is wonderful and Aspot is a busy but happy man. A couple months later Aspot's new mother-in-law comes to visit for a week to give care for the children of his new brother-in-law while his new sister-in-law gives birth. However, weeks later the mother-in-law is still visiting and beginning to rearrange their home in a fashion which begins to concern Aspot.

Nevertheless, Life is good, his wife is delightful and happy and there is no shadow too dark that he cannot find a way to peek over.

Fiery Darts

Their home is now conveniently adjacent to one of the many Denver bicycle paths and although his daily bicycle commute is now a bit longer it is also a much better route. Part of this new path includes a sidewalk which ends into a dirt path created mostly by wildlife, such as coyotes, often spotted watching him approach before they silently retreat away into deep weeds and out of sight. At this time he is helping better define this coyote path being widened by repeated usage as his tires crush many weeds everywhere about this commuting shortcut that seems oddly unused by anyone else. Well, to be honest, it is not odd when considering the paddle locked gates he has to crawl across. Oops...it seems he might be offering some type of confession...

A fuller picture of this shortcut is that there is an unused Denver 425 turnpike overpass that obviously was built many years earlier. This overpass probably gets but very little notice from the turnpike traffic flowing under it because very few people are aware that this aging overpass has, most likely, never been used. Well, unused until very recent, because it is closed by rusted paddle-locked gates, but of which Aspot is willing to twice daily lift his bike over and say "Thank you!" without feeling guilt. "Why, no guilt?" you might ask.

Well first of all the south end opens into a large unmaintained end of a suburb city park. And secondly the north end abruptly terminates broadside against a possibly ill planned, townhome community which does not show evidence of any intent for a street ever being connected to this overpass. Furthermore, neither end has any "No Trespassing" signage posted. Last, but not least, this overpass, was most likely built and paid for by taxpayers, of which Aspot is most certainly a member who questions the purpose of an overpass built only for coyotes? Therefore because this shortcut saves him miles of riding every day and offers a peacefully pleasant relief from the otherwise frantic street-side route which does absolutely no harm to anyone by his use of it during his work commute. He feels absolutely no remorse for making good use of otherwise wasted world resources and tax dollars.

The newly married couple enjoy early September. Yet three days earlier he had been startled awake in the middle of the night and had taken comfort from the close proximity of his wife who was still peacefully sleeping as he had pondered a vivid dream of stark intensity. He ponders the meaning of this dream, its incredible clarity and remains sleepless for hours until she awakens at which time he gently asks "Honey, are you awake enough for me to share something that feels important?" at which she sits up higher and nods a yes while resting her cheek on his shoulder. He proceeds to say "I believe our country is going to be physically attacked by an external armed force".

It has been three days since that dream and today is, yet, of little interest to anyone but, perhaps, the somewhat sleepy passengers anxious to reach loved ones or tasks at the end of their forthcoming air-rides as they wait in seats of multi-passenger airliners, possibly even now on taxiways for takeoff. Aspot is singing while he bicycle commutes to work as the sun just starts to poke above the eastern horizon with the weather of a seemingly perfect morning.

As Aspot rapidly approaches the end of the sidewalk to enter the coyote path, he quickly determines that this day is rather peculiar, because as he approaches the end of the sidewalk he has to suddenly brake hard and slide his bike to a stop to avoid puncturing his tires upon many sharp screws spread widely across the end of the sidewalk and the entry to the coyote path.

"What is this?" he exclaims, as he begins to scan the situation and perceives an obvious attempt to sabotage the path. The screws are scattered in a circular pattern about eight feet in diameter across the sidewalk and out into the dirt. He shakes his head and says "Nice gift!" The reason he says "gift" is because he commonly uses similar hardware and eyes these sabotage purposed screws as freebies for common bench-stock use at his workshop at home and so begins to gather them into a large empty pouch of his backpack. There are actually two different kinds of screws, one is a very short, self-piercing sheet-metal type of screw with rather broad heads that sit straight up easily, while the other screw is a very short, sharp, drywall type. There seems to be about an equal number of both types being collected.

As he continues to individually pick up the many screws a strange feeling begins to creep up his spine, causing him to quickly stand and say "Now this is really weird." because he has noticed that these screws have <u>not</u>

been randomly scattered but rather were carefully and very evenly distributed. In fact they seem so precisely placed that not one of these screws touches another but rather they are all evenly distributed with equal spacing between each of alternating types.

This fact might not be all that interesting if there were but a few screws, but by the time he finished he has filled a large pouch containing nearly four pounds of them which is hundreds of screws. He considers the amount of time and effort, it had required, to so precisely place them this way. Whoever had sabotaged this bike path had laid out these screws with an amazing amount of pre-mediated intent and sheer determination that is bordering seeming madness. Now standing and staring at this scene in total amazement he audibly and loudly exclaims "Wow!"

The strangeness of this bizarre encounter has, by this time, become quite uncomfortable and a chill drives deeply into his bones, so that he drops to his knees asking God to dispel the spirit. It is then, very softly, he hears "demons" and responding with a nod says "Yes Lord, the demons were busy last night!" But now feeling the presence of the Holy Spirit, he is calmed and continues to quickly gather the remaining screws. But again he is stopped to wonder if this maze of screws might have been deposited with some type of intentional pattern within the contrast of varying screw types? But he has already gathered too many to discern a specific pattern and so if there had been an embedded image, it has already been lost.

After commuting the remaining miles to work and taking his usual post commute shower he bounds up the stairs and enters the work area which has numerous engineering cubicles where software developers generally are found individually working upon development of various products. However this morning he notices many co-workers are crowded together and quietly staring at a TV in one of the closest cubicles.

"Hey, what's up?" he asks. Someone replies, "A jetliner just flew into one of the World Trade Center buildings a bit ago. It is believed to have been done by a terrorist".

He joins the cluster as they listen to the news broadcast and watch the camera scan the smoking building. Suddenly the camera swings to focus upon a second airplane just a moment before it plunges into the second building. In an instant he realizes that he has already seen and described this very event, to his wife, only three days earlier.

Even though it was only, at that time, but a dream, it was also one of those where even though you are sleeping you are also well aware of being asleep, but awake within a dream. Furthermore, Aspot knew that he was not alone in this dream because he was told, as it began, "Pay attention, I have something to tell you" This dreamed event as shared with his wife three days earlier follows:

Aspot finds himself standing in the middle of a street, with familiar houses, and so he perceives that he is somewhere within the neighborhood at which he currently lives. It seems an overcast day with the sky a heavy dark grey. In the near distance he spots two very tall strange buildings which are quite out of place for his neighborhood and they are certainly of an unknown purpose. Curiosity asks him to walk towards them and understand what they mean and why they are now present in his neighborhood. Perhaps these are new high-rise condominiums he wonders and his focus is fixed upon them. He cannot discern their distance from him because he continues to walk quite a distance, some number of city blocks, but yet these two buildings seem to stay just as far away. This is really quite odd he thinks and walks faster to try and catch up with them.

Out of the corner of his left eye his attention is caught by an object flying in the air above, it seems little more than block away to the left and about a football field over his head. The object, emitting a trail of smoke, is flying so slow that he wonders how it stays aloft and does not fall down. It is difficult to see it clearly because of the dark gray background but it is most certainly cylindrical and appears that it might have short wings. He wonders what this object might be and senses it to be an ill purposed type of missile which although its shape is rather poorly defined is definitely casting some amount of flame. But being unable to discern what kind of vehicle it might he declares aloud, within his dream, "A fiery dart!"

It is greatly perplexing how it can fly so slow and not just fall down. It is as if that thing is simply hanging from a string he thinks. Nevertheless, this fiery dart is going faster than he is walking and perhaps, by coincidence seems to be traveling the same direction he is going. Shortly in fact it seems certainly aimed towards those two tall buildings still standing far before him.

A second flying object is now noticed to be approaching overhead on the other side of him. It is similar in every fashion as the first one and also heading the same direction.

Now feeling a sense of disaster and urgency he starts running towards the two tall buildings. With little surprise, but yet terror, he watches the first fiery dart strike the top of one the two tall buildings. He sees a great explosion and a black cloud spewing angrily from the top of that building and he believes this to be the beginning of a prolonged enemy attack.

Then another fear, if not horror, comes to heart in concern for the safety of his wife and his interest in the tall buildings immediately diminishes as he spins around to run towards home. Soon behind him now behind him comes the expected sound of a second explosion but he does not take time to look because his focus is now only upon safety of his wife and others in the neighborhood.

Nearly out of breath by the time he reaches the door at home, he shouts loudly "Honey, take cover we are being attacked by an enemy!" but not finding his wife in the house so runs back outside where he spots three persons walking side-by-side directly towards him. While yet feeling the urgency of an enemy attack on the neighborhood his attention is oddly and strongly drawn towards the three people. At first feeling inclined to shout them a warning about the enemy attack, he rather senses an even greater evil emanating from them which strictly shuts his mouth. In fact he senses that they are now a bigger threat to his family and so trots quickly towards them to intersect them from reaching his home as soon as is possible.

Now being about five car lengths apart two of them stop walking but the third continues to proceed and at this time Aspot recognizes a familiar smile ... (this portion of the dream was not shared with his wife for easily understandable reason) ... the smile of his father-in-law who, seems oblivious about the danger of fiery darts. Rather his father-in-law shows a desire to start a casual chat, which annoys Aspot who exclaims "Did you not see that great explosion?!" pointing across his shoulder towards the much smoke in the distance. The father-in-law shows no concern and turns to respect the middle person who again is approaching. This middle person, a man, wearing a well fitted and tailored suit, presents himself now as if bearing some form of authority. Aspot recognizes the evil Ha'satan immediately, but all identity of third person of the group remains obscured.

With no facial expression, Ha'satan calmly asks "Do you think those explosions are impressive?" and then after a short pause continues to say "They are nothing compared to what is coming.", "I cause fires." and points towards the Aspot's home. "See i start one even now" In an instant flames begin to show from Aspot's basement windows. "No! My son is down there and you cannot harm him!" At which Ha'satan replies "Then I guess you had better protect him."

Aspot dashes toward the house and sees a stairway suddenly show in the lawn which appears that Providence has purposefully created solely for the exit of his son from the basement. And indeed even before he reaches the stairs his son darts up them unscathed by fire.

It was at this point that Aspot, greatly startled, had awakened from that dream. But, it is now three days later and he is watching life being crushed as the towers crumble and drop, in a plume of smoking debris, right before the very eyes of this nation and the world.

The hair on the back of his neck rises with a deep spirited chill as he instantly understands the reason why the fiery darts seemed to be barely moving, in the air, during his dream. It is because in the dream he did not comprehend the scale of the setting, that is to say, the size or distance of either the two tall buildings or fiery darts. The fiery darts, which he perceived to be moving extremely slow, were of a far unknown distance and actually travelling hundreds of miles an hour.

Well, we know the rest of this story... or do we? What was meant, in that dream, when Ha'satan indicated that the collapsing towers "are nothing compared to what is coming"? And is it possible that those, seemingly demonized bike trail sabotage screws, this same morning, are in some fashion related? If so, then we must ask, for what reason? Is it possible the closer we walk with God, the thinner the veil between the spiritual and physical world becomes? It seems to be a part of the mystery about the war between good and evil … Is our (mankind's) Life at stake …? A battle is most certainly waging and perhaps in most subtle manners we do not expect or consider …

After work and back at home, Aspot finds it rather curious, if not odd, that his wife does not show any interest in discussing the actual 9/11 incident with him. Perhaps she is too preoccupied with her mother who continues to extend a so-called 'brief visit' far too long.

4

FOLDING STEEL

Sometimes life just makes a wild, unexpected turn without providing any advance notice.

Mad Cows

In fact, Aspot and his new bride do not really get to know one another, before the mother-in-law comes to visit and does not leave. Rather she continues to provide an array of excuses for having missed her return flight to where her husband, now on a missionary journey, is located. Four months later it is quite apparent that her excuses are empty and that she has no intention of ever leaving. This still might have worked out well if the mother-in-law had shown an ounce of love in her heart, but this mother-in-law does not.

This is indeed showing to be a season of much unexpected frustration, primarily because of intense interference and unrest being directly sown between Aspot and his new wife from inside their new home. In fact, it was quickly becoming obvious, that the mother-in-law seems to be trying to break his marriage apart by such things a holding a garage sale and selling Aspot's music collection while he was at work and many other similar things. Yet Aspot continues to hold his tongue because he knows that God is working with him and attempting to show him something important.

In fact, it is also a season of much spiritual growth and increasing communication with the Holy Spirit. This is a season of extreme personal spiritual providence ... faith is a gift, take hold and hold tightly ... Perhaps re-examine our experiences with God ...

Daily the work commute is still by bicycle, in all types of weather of all seasons, but not for the purpose of physical health. Rather he continues to ride the bicycle to work because he truly appreciates the peace of the bicycle paths in contrast to stress of mainstream and rush-hour traffic. Furthermore he enjoys 'riding with God' and loudly sings songs of worship of either well know favorites or spontaneous new songs. The joy of the Spirit is in his heart!

Riding with God

But now, everywhere in this nation, that proclaims "In God we Trust", the zeal of the American spirit is still high, following the 911 wakeup and it is by chance that a street block of his work commute accompanies alongside a tall steel fence surrounding none other but a Muslim masque. The building inside this fence never catches much of his attention or interest, even now, because he has never seen any activity inside this fence beyond, at times, one or two vehicles sitting in its parking lot. He has never seen any people inside the fence and as best he can tell this masque is not getting any attendance. This is a comfortable observation and makes this masque little more than an artifact of loose association with the very recent 9/11/2001 historical mishap.

Prayer is a habit, learned early as a child and he prays as he bicycles to work and it seems, Love (God) is showing him through life and in increasingly greater frequency, what seems to be, meaningful … in part by the manner things work in life and in part … Spiritual … dreams.

For instance; he dreams to be walking down the street past this masque and upon his shoulders he carries a young boy about the age of five. After passing the masque they approach a short arched bridge, (which does not exist in the real) with many persons milling about and crossing the bridge ahead of him. They are all wearing what resemble African style garments, of loose hanging cloth and brightly colored. The women are all wearing shawls and moving in distinct small groups with many children.

As he and the boy come close to this crowd many of them begin to show an uncomfortable interest in their presence to the extent that some of the older children in the crowd began to yell, make angry shouts and raise fists towards Aspot and the boy. In fact the entire crowd becomes exceedingly excited and angry. Aspot tries to push fast through the crowd which seems now to be an angry mob surrounding Aspot and the boy as they continue to cross the bridge.

A number of the Muslim boys are seen to stoop alongside both ends of the bridge and gather handfuls of mud, then run close and throw it directly towards Aspot and the boy. Aspot quickly realizes that they are not aiming at him but rather their anger and aim is at the boy who is yet riding upon his shoulders. In fact the boy becomes quickly covered in dark muddy goo.

With dismay, Aspot feels ashamed for letting the boy he carries being so coarsely abused. But when he looks upward into the boy's muddy face the boy speaks, saying "Do not worry about me. I am fine", "Watch this" Suddenly the boy's face become clean and his clothes a dazzling white. At this time Aspot realizes the Boy is actually our yet young Lord Jesus. The crowd seems stunned by how His clothes instantly became brilliant white and His face radiantly clean and joyful. In fact the crowd becomes quiet and backs away. Now still with young Jesus smiling and riding on his shoulders they continue without further provocation across the bridge.

At this point Aspot awakes from the dream and lays for a while recalling the intensity of the dream and pondering what it might mean. Then he prepares for and begins his daily bicycle commute. Still pondering the dream and knowing that he will soon turn a corner and go past the Muslim masque seen in this dream he does not expect to see anyone in the compound and begins as normal to sing a contemporary Christian song.

However this day as he comes around the corner he immediately sees a large crowd of persons milling and walking in distinct small groups with many children. The garments of the crowd are predominantly brightly colored African style garments, with women wearing shawls over their heads. That dream is become alive in the real and neck hairs stand as a chill cools his spine. It appears as if there has been a very early morning or night Muslim service at the masque and that now the crowd is taking a break and crossing the street in large numbers towards a mid-eastern deli/café.

A sudden chill quickly dispels as he recalls the outcome of the dream and resumes singing even louder as he pedals and weaves, without concern, through this crowd, while also knowing that in some fashion, unseen by everyone else, upon his shoulders is riding the eternal Christ, yet a boy, brightly smiling and peacefully wearing brilliant dazzling white garments!

BTW; this is both the first and last time Aspot ever seen any of that Muslim crowd.

Children knocking

A voice speaks to him while yet asleep and says "See this" Within a dream he sees a bed before him and upon it is his wife is lying with another man. In the dream he hears "You will not know any further intimacy with your wife". Aspot awakens, observes his wife beside him sleeping peacefully, and gets up to find calm rather than the ill feel of this dream. He sits and reads the Bible.

A second night later, again sleeping he hears, "See this". Standing at the entry door are a young boy and a girl, of six or seven, knocking and calling "Mom!" Through the window he could see his wife sitting in a chair reading and ignoring the calls of the two children which Aspot knows to be the two children they are soon to finish adopting. Again, waking, as out of a nightmare, much troubled Aspot gets up and goes to work early while praying the entire commute.

During this same day he receives a phone call, from his closest neighbor, who is reporting having observed Aspot's father-in-law lifting Aspot's dog off the ground, by its collar, and while this dog was gasping for breath the father-in-law was maliciously kicking the dog. This neighbor lets Aspot know that if he ever again sees such animal mistreatment he will immediately call the police.

Aspot wishes his neighbor had called the police rather than leaving the issue for him to work out with his father-in-law. This same evening Aspot attempts to discuss this issue with his father-in-law which does become a heated angry argument regarding not just the ill treatment of his dog but also the much other abuse and ongoing attacks that would be detrimental to any marriage. That night the mother-in-law escorts Aspot's wife silently away, to live, distant with her brother.

Sigh ... Yet we Praise God who remains with us through our darkest hours!

Perhaps, those who find it easy to show the deepest form of love are the same ones who find it most easy to drop to the bottomless depths when love is lost? Perhaps, there is a time when, we need to think love is lost so that we might search for and find the true Love of God.

Eclipse

Months later, his wife still has not returned and Aspot's eyes are now intently focused upon the stoplight directly ahead, Aspot is balancing, posed, without motion upon both bicycle pedals, braced, with a firm grip of both handlebars, eager for this inconvenient commuter traffic light to turn green. Behind him an angry automobile impatiently revs its engine and feigns a brake-constrained lurch toward him as if wishing to crush his tail, but Aspot does not flinch nor seem to take notice because his mind is not here but rather distant with much hope for meeting his wife. You see earlier that day, his father-in-law called to arrange a meeting for Aspot and his estranged wife. This came as a great and encouraging surprise, because he has not been able to contact her for months.

But now he is riding towards a coffee shop near his home where he will meet his lovely wife and already, in his mind, he pictures her waiting at a coffee shop table to meet him. Possibly she is enjoying a novel to kill time as she awaits his arrival. There are many contrary things he could also be thinking but he chooses to consider his wife in only the brightest manner because he loves her, deeply misses her smile and at this moment nothing else matters!

The spastic auto behind revs it engine again even as the light ahead turns green. Without hesitation Aspot's has his fullest attention back on the task of bicycling to the coffee shop. His back arches and muscles extend as he applies full leg strength to the pedal. Tension binds the chain tightly to wheel and the bicycle obediently responds and jumps forward.

But suddenly Aspot hears a sharp metallic sound of snapping metal and from the corner of eye sees a pedal and broken crank-arm go dancing in a reckless careen across the street. This same instant his foot unexpectedly extends far beyond the anticipated stroke and with his motion being caught off guard his body assumes an absurd sideways list. Reflex responds much faster than mental comprehension and prevents his head from hitting pavement directly in front of that impatient car now rapidly accelerating alarmingly close behind him.

Landing, awkwardly but somewhat upright, Aspot punches the pavement with the one free leg and pushes himself backwards to miss being struck by that automobile which also makes a wild evasive swerve. Hearing the squealing of tires, he lands backward on the pavement beneath a thick cloud of exhaust. With a grunt he quickly yanks his bike out of the way of remaining traffic and begins to survey the situation. His heart groans under the plight of this wicked situation which instantly taunts him "You are going to miss meeting your wife!"

The initial shock hits him hard and he glares angrily at the remaining stub of the pedal arm. Glancing at his watch he accepts the fact that he has exactly forty minutes to reach the coffee shop. Ok this would normally be plenty of time to bicycle the remaining ten miles. But the basic fact is that he now has no form of transportation! So his mind starts racing madly to find some way of letting his wife know that he is having difficulty in to getting to meet her the way he most truly desires at the coffee shop!

Ok, believe it or not, there once was 'a time before cell phones' and Aspot does not have a cell phone. However it is yet a time that he can find a pay phone at the closest convenience store, two miles ahead, but then he does not know his wife's current phone number. And although his father-in-law's did call him earlier, that call came to his desk phone, it is now two miles behind and it does not provide caller-id history anyway. So he does not have any means of directly or indirectly contacting her by phone aside from possibly calling the coffee shop.

Calling the coffee shop, itself, seems to be the best option but it is far from perfect, because it is also a large deli which probably means reaching someone who is probably busy and most certainly does not even know his wife. So then asking them to either broadcast a message to her by name or go search for her is not promising. Furthermore he must first find out the name and phone number of that coffee shop, which he can only most certainly determine at work, two miles behind him.

Maybe put up a thumb and hitch it? No, this is very unlikely, because he is currently located in an area only now developing and traffic is very minimal. Besides finding someone to give him a ride going even somewhat in the needed direction would defy statistical odds because there is a huge water reservoir between this location and the coffee shop. Furthermore all around the reservoir is a great maze of streets often blocked by unexpected diagonally running routes, the result of many years of unchecked early suburban sprawl. With this knowledge in mind hitchhiking seems only a grave waste of the very little and precious time!

Ok, he is familiar with public transportation and knows many of the local bus stops which run every thirty minutes but quickly dismisses this idea because he also knows that it takes three busses to get home which takes an additional hour after he gets to the closest bus stop. The fastest transportation is by cab, but the time it takes to even reach a phone in either direction, will be about the same time she is expecting to see him.

He just needs to get back to work as quickly as possible, call both a cab and the coffee shop. Turning around he sets a rapid pace, pushing his bicycle in the opposite direction his heart so strongly desires to be going. He pictures his wife, resolute, sitting, waiting… elbows on table, chin wistfully in hands, waiting… waiting and can image her, thinking that he, by not showing up, does not care, and so with a sigh leaving the coffee shop…

About him a slight breeze causes the blossoms of tall wild alfalfa wave at him but this is little noticed, while he pushes the useless bicycle, feeling the fullest gravity of the problem and overwhelmed by the certainty of missing his only chance of meeting his love before she decides to permanently disappear from his life. His chance to see her is come so close yet by some cruel trick has become seemingly impossible to touch!

A tear wants to form but he fights it and instead starts to call himself names and asks himself, why with this meeting being so very important, he had not obtained some type of phone number? Why had he not considered transportation problems? Was it really necessary for his well-maintained and usually dependable bicycle to break in a manner he has no means of fixing, at the most incredibly inconvenient of times. These and a litany of other thoughts are severely beating him.

Dark clouds take command as he bears the weight of the pending certain impossibility of meeting his wife before she grows weary and leaves the coffee shop never knowing why he did not show. His shoulders slump as he considers a final surrender in the fight for his marriage that has already become like over-stretched barbed wire.

"Hey!", "Are you forgetting something?" He hears an inner voice but refuses to listen to it. Rather he shakes his head and silently mutters, "No", "Love has lost".

"Are you sure?"

He doesn't pause from his fast paced walk yet feels a slight tug from the emerging subtle truth. Regardless of how impossible it seems, faith is again asking him to consider the impossible. Even now with less than thirty minutes remaining to reach that coffee shop he is moved to consider; If Father in Heaven wills it then anything is possible. So with a certain nod and an earnest look upward, while yet rapidly pushing his bicycle the wrong direction, he deposits into the wind this prayer, "Papa, I am placing my need to reach this meeting into your hands".

The gentle breeze now dances atop the alfalfa blossoms and no more than thirty seconds later a pickup truck slows to a stop alongside him and the window rolls down, whereupon the driver yells at him through the cab, "Need a ride?"

"Well yes ... Thank you, but we are both most obviously travelling south and as difficult as it might seem, at this time, I am actually trying to go north.

The driver of the truck heartily chuckles then says "Well as difficult as it might also appear to you, so am I!", "Throw your bike in the back and get in."

His heart and mind races as he eagerly responds, "Most definitely", even while already swinging the bicycle into the back of the truck.

As soon as Aspot hops into the cab of the stranger's truck, the driver quickly continues down the road a short distance, pulls into a parking lot of a credit union and walks to its door. Shortly the driver gets back into the cab says, "I am here only to deposit my son's paycheck but his bank is closed.", "Well then I guess, I am really only here to give you a ride", then exiting the parking lot his truck heads north. The stranger adds "I might not get you exactly where you want to go, but I can at least get you closer than you are now.", "So tell me where you are headed so that I might know the best place to drop you off?" But when Aspot mentions the coffee shop deli at corner of Alameda and Chambers" the stranger laughs and replies, "Oh, how convenient for both of us, I only live a block from there"

This is almost unbelievably promising news, Aspot's spirit rises greatly and they engage in a light hearted discussion with ample levity as stoplights and traffic condition prove to be abnormally agreeable. After an unexpectedly short ride, Aspot gets out the truck right in front of the coffee shop, humbled, joyful and eager to meet his estranged wife exactly on time.

However as he approaches he sees his father-in-law sitting at a patio table but not his wife. There is a pronounced and disturbingly grave tone of his father-in-law's face that quickly causes the joyful excitement of his heart to become immediately squelched. Sensing a need for caution Aspot carefully asks, his father-in-law, while scanning through the window, "Is my wife inside?" He hears a somber "No".

He feels a moment of unbalance, vertigo, as his hope immediately plummets Nevertheless, needing to discuss the situation with his father-in-law, Aspot pulls out a chair to talk, but his father-in-law quickly stands holding a to-go coffee cup, making it inherently clear this is to be a very short meeting with him alone. The father-in-law says "Your marriage to my daughter is over." "But you need to consider how you are going to divvy up your finances with her". This statement came as a sidewise blow, in part, because of how Aspot had been told this meeting was to be with his wife as a step towards healing their marriage. But even more so because only minutes earlier Aspot was greatly encouraged, riding in a truck, absolutely certain that God was making it possible for him to meet with his wife.

Therefore although he can hear his father-in-law babbling about providing financial records and bank statements his heart and mind are far elsewhere, reeling with emotion coming from many angles. Through the fog of the moment Aspot abruptly cuts the monologue of his father-in-law short by saying "First of all, the concerns of my marriage are between my wife and me, not you". "Secondly, I am sure God is willing to work my wife and I through our problems, which mainly stem from having meddlesome parents in our home"

In short, nothing good came from this ill-formed meeting. So then, why the pleasant, blessed ride with the elderly man, who intending to assist his son, had, instead only, helped Aspot reach this destination? Aspot prays

"Father please help me understand why you helped get me to this coffee shop". He does not know if he got an answer because of much noise and turmoil in his heart. And although, Aspot has found little comprehension as to why he was so well helped get to that ill-formed meeting he still gives thanks to the God, he loves, but of whom he obviously does not fully understand.

Mercy!

His heart is broken while still greatly missing his wife. Life is become cold, harsh ... sleepless ... without melody ... it feels as if he is, yet again, being deeply plowed ... long after he had hoped, even begin to think that plowing had been finished ... and the 'seed well planted', even already growing ... but ... is this the plow again or something different?

There are a number of rather deep and heartfelt dialogues between God and Aspot at this time and to be honest, anger is exchanged, largely because another man, a clergyman, behind the curtain has entered the story and became a catastrophic wedge between Aspot and Aspot's wife. There is little need to delve into the tawdry details of this strange third party relationship because many of us are all already much too familiar with the taste of this rather insidious malady. Nevertheless, the role and manner in which this intruder enters the scene seems of importance to God by the extent in which we are soon to see, within the Life of Aspot, even greater more tangible, personal interactions with Love (God). The stark reality (divorce decree delivered and in hand) that his wife is permanently gone have crystalized Aspot's realization of

God's importance and companionship! At times he truly does not know whether to laugh or cry … so does both …

Furthermore this affair has succinctly catalyzed the focus of Aspot's biologically spiritual eye which, now, while continuing to look up is also acutely observing, studying and trying to understand 'The Church'.

Love whispers … "There is purpose" …

5

FORMING SHAPE

It can easily be claimed, that perhaps a bit 'under the table', Aspot has been being guided by the same mysterious God of which he has been diligently searching for. Yes, Aspot can often feel and even at times see God's presence, yet it seems that God is always just one step too far ahead to really catch a fully definitive outline of what He truly looks like. But then does it really matter what God looks like, as we work our way through daily life? Isn't it important what our spouse looks like even though we work individually each day of life?

We know it is true that there is much more to 'looks' than what meets the eye. For example, within any relationship, over time we develop an understanding that allows us to know when and to what degree we can trust that our back is being defended by those near to us. This is one type of 'looks' that pertains more to our spouse than anyone else. What God looks like does matter and within this sensibility follows the basis for which we begin to develop a better understanding about who He is and thereby learn to walk more like Him, which in essence what it means to be "in Him" and "in His name".

Beside, were we not created in the image of God? Is this the image others see of one another? Is this the image of our spouse? Should it be? Can it be? If we listen we will surely hear God say "Yes" and "Yes"? It is important we can recognize whom we are with and/or following.

But, we now rejoin the story of Life with Aspot and are stepping into a journey, already in motion, which is an important witness account of God's heart, which we want to follow, tangibly exposed and in motion. We continue to follow ...

There is also a third church, of a totally different faith, within this city that Aspot much wants to visit. It is street mission, an evangelical church and actually the reason why he chose to start his journey here in the northern part of the state rather than in southern end where the main office of the bishop is located. Aspot knows about this evangelical church by the report of a wonderful man, an uncle, who is a carpenter by trade. His uncle has previously shared a recount of an amazing experience that he had in this church while he had, while remotely working upon a building project, some years earlier.

He had reported that this modest non-descript congregation, gathered under an evangelical fellowship billboard, of a vacated store, within the middle of an old city block. The reason this church is important to Aspot is because his uncle had reported that parishioners have come to expect for the Holy Spirit, at times, to anoint phrases or portions of a page within their bibles with sweet smelling oil. His uncle had only just happened to attend this church because it was conveniently close to his job site for a few Sundays.

It was during one of these Sunday visits that his uncle found out about the bible anointing when some portion of parishioners made it known to the entire congregation that they had been blessed by an anointing visit of God that had left an oil mark somewhere on the pages of their bible. So his uncle upon hearing this news searched his bible and found one spot in his bible that had been anointed, highlighted with oil. Later he showed Aspot his bible and the anointed spot still maintained a sweet smelling aroma. The much enthusiasm of his uncle was sincere and since that time Aspot has been eager to visit this church with his bible. So this morning, with his favorite bible in hand, he plans to locate and attend the Sunday service of this ministry.

Having located this church, by its street side billboard, he enters, is warmly greeted and directed up on old flight of wooden stairs into what might have once been an upper level store or possibly product-storage of a store, below, at street level. This upper room is large and well windowed with chairs for seating about two hundred people. At the far end from the stairs can be seen a modest alter. Sunshine is coming in brightly through the large old windows so that the entire church floor is well lit.

Persons meander in and sit down, rather sparsely and which seemed to imply there being little personal relationship between most of the parishioners which is not surprising for an evangelical ministry that is primarily focused upon serving, often haggard looking, street persons. Indeed there is noticeable contrast among the parishioners as they shuffle and take a seat. Some do look like they live in a home, well showered and groomed. While others have an ill-kept appearance and look like they might have actually woke up inside a box, within some nearby alley only minutes earlier. Nonetheless, he watches most, if not all, parishioners to be carrying a bible as they come into the room and sit down in a random fashion.

To the left of Aspot a humble looking man sits down leaving an empty chair between himself and Aspot. Not long after, a woman with clean but well-worn attire approaches and extends a warm hello to Aspot as she takes a seat on the right side of him. By the time the pastor, an older man, shows, the church is about one-third full and this seems to be about as full as it is going to get. An old hymn starts the service and then the pastor reads a gospel verse and begins to speak. Aspot's attention is but loosely attentive to the sermon because he is being tugged by the feel of the presence of the spirit in the persons all around him. Yet, he does take notice the pastor's keen focus on the scripture and how he skillfully illustrates a less obvious, subtle meaning of the verse.

But when the pastor seems satisfied that he has adequately illustrated the verse from the Word he stops talking for a moment and looks rather distracted as if pondering. Then he looks up scans the sheep in the seats before him and continues. "There is something that most of you don't know about me and this feels like a good time to discuss it, because it touches upon a topic very dear to me.", "In the past I was a priest and everyone called me Father..."

Aspot becomes quickly riveted to this part of pastor's sermon because it is touching very close to a greater topic related of why he is today in California. As he continues to listen, it begins to seem as if this pastor has probed his heart and touching upon the main reason for his journey. Aspot's attention is become keenly focused upon the words of this pastor who does not dwell long on the topic but makes it known that the churches of the 'Catholic' variety (Believe it or not, not all Catholic churches are Roman) that he had been a priest of, was in ancient times very true to God but "has become corrupt" and now "its heart is not with God".

"Wow!" Aspot mutters, because this sermon is harmonizing, amazingly well, with the primary reason Aspot is taking this trip to California … (Hint to Reader: God moves like God and NOT like we do … the Holy Spirit is moving but NOT the way Aspot is at this moment thinking … even though …)

As the pastor is wrapping up his personal disclosure … parishioners begin to jump up from their chairs, shout and making much loud noise. "Halleluiah!", "Lord! Lord! Lord!" It takes less than a moment before Aspot can see the cause of their loud out-cries, and is made utterly speechless …

Parishioners are raising their bibles high to show an opaque light fragrant oil splatter from the pages of the bibles to their brows, beards, garment hems and shoes. Some bibles can only be seen to be dripping but others shower this opaque oil as if from a lively spring rain. Still others can be seen to pouring a stream of oil as if the pages contain a water faucet turned fully on! Furthermore oil can be seen dripping from along the entire edge of the altar. Additionally some if not all windows become obscure and seen dripping oil from the sills. Aspot cannot stand still any longer and goes to look closer at a window and by visual inspection discovers that oil has spread across and flowing in a very thin film down the much of the entire window pane.

This outpouring and is nothing short of a miracle. It is a totally awesome and amazing experience. Aspot is absorbing the moment, the excitement and the pronounced sweet aroma and this wonderful kiss from God.

Aspot runs to the Alter, kneels and opens palms of his hand to capture holy oil, letting it heavily drip onto his scalp and into his beard. This holy oil is indeed the source of the now much sweet smelling fragrance. Aspot scans the room and the much commotion of the sheep. There is no way to fully describe, illustrate or convey awe, the wonder of this miraculous experience and the presence of God.

The explicit visual presence of God does not last long and shortly the bibles stop raining oil, the altar again stands still and the windows lift their veil. The pastor now loudly says, "Praise the Lord! The Holy Spirit is with us very strong today! Let us take the opportunity to spend time with the Holy Spirit." It is a Holy time. Everyone shows some amount of sincere time with God, many standing or sitting with heads bowed or raised. Others drop to their knees.

As for Aspot, he is, at this moment, quite certain that God is standing in support of his primary mission to California … However … After some minutes a low murmur begins to be heard as parishioners begin to share and discuss with one another. Aspot starts examining his bible, hoping to find specific and personal guidance from God by oil anointing upon the Word of his bible. But he cannot find even any faintest mark of oil.

The gentleman sitting to the left, watches Aspot search and after a while says, "My bible has been anointed in Ezekiel 13:9". The woman on his right side then quickly asserts, "My bible is also anointed at Ezekiel 13:9"! A short discussion about Ezekiel 13:9 follows and it begins to seem the parishioners on both sides of him are giving him looks of suspicion. Aspot says little, possibly because he is indeed feeling shame as Ezekiel 13:9 is coming at him from both sides. But mainly he is quiet because he perceives this verse as being, at this time, very direct guidance, pertaining to his mission in California and is now listening intently to discern the possible voice of the Holy Spirit.

The atmosphere is silent but heavy with a feeling of the Holy Spirit being very near... Close enough to feel the very heartbeat of God... Love...

Brothers

"When you can embrace... "

Aspot prays but hears nothing, so proceeds to travel south towards the city of the main office of the bishop whom manages the clergyman, the final lynch pin of his recent divorce. In prayer Aspot asks "Father, what are you trying to show me?" It seems, not by chance, that the bibles of the strangers sitting next to him in the church, one to the left and the other to the right side of him both had their bibles highlighted with oil on the same verse.

Yes he is strongly feeling a "Whoa there horsy" from the Spirit but is confused, because in his heart, the behavior of a certain priest which resulted in the loss of his wife is very heavy on his heart. It still seems important to discuss this with that priest's superior. "Lord what will you have me consider?"

Back roads are his preference and so he follows narrow roads through the hills of California and stops at a couple of local farmers roadside stands to obtain fruit and nuts to snack on. He examines the lovely farms, the countryside and continues to pray. And then the Holy Spirit speaks:

"Did I ask you to discuss your concern with anyone aside from the priest?", "Did I tell you to travel anywhere?", "Rather you do this thing of your will and not mine." and "It is well you understand my way."

There is little doubt that the Holy Spirit is expressively trouncing Aspot's intended discussion with the bishop, which greatly perplexes him and so he implores with God "But Lord, is it ok for people who have faith in you to be misled by your Church elders and, at times, even be harmed by a ruthlessly abusive elder?" The Holy Spirit responds with a simple, somber and lingering "No".

Aspot remains perplexed and ponders the dilemma and the much he has experienced through the ordeal of losing his wife and today. He pulls off to the side of the road, parks the car, sits, ponders and prays. He does not continue towards Los Angelis to speak with the bishop, but cannot understand why he has been stopped. He gets out of the car and enters a non-fenced grove of fruit trees and walks in prayerful mediation. As the shadows of the day start to become long the Holy Spirit eventually speaks again and tells him;

"When you can embrace, as a brother, the man you accuse, then you have done well!"

Aspot is not yet aware that the discussion is already over. "Embrace as brothers?", "What do you mean?", "Brother?", "That man pretends to be a priest so he can mercilessly destroy my life and take my wife from me?", "It seems that if he could he would totally annihilate me!", "What has he done to other people?" The Holy Spirit remains quiet as Aspot rants.

As the dark of night takes hold of the day Aspot finally wanders back to his rental car still mumbling "When I can embrace him as a brother ... what does this mean?"

In any case, Aspot has no intention of disregarding direct guidance from God. So he changes his course and heads early towards a loved and aging aunt who lives not far.

"Embrace as a brother" ... ?

Balance

It is elk bow hunting season. Aspot and one of his sibling brothers have taken time off from work to walk with stealth and bows in the mountains. The second day out they encounter a herd of elk, broadside to their approach, less than thirty yards away. Aspot's brother is in the lead, has bow with arrow positioned and has the first choice of targets. Aspot also has his arrow pulled for release but is waiting for his brother to cast first. Suddenly the elk take notice of the hunters and quickly disappear.

Aspot asks, "Hey, why didn't you shoot?"

"My release refused to open. Why didn't you shoot?"

"Well, because you were leading and had first choice."

"Don't matter, when I didn't let my arrow fly, you should have." Both brothers laugh and carry on. They did not encounter any further elk that day but set tents for the night eager to try again the next day.

However, this night, as Aspot sleeps, he hears that his help is needed at the pony-tailed priest's church and is immediately awoken to consider what he has just been told. Very early the next morning he tells his brother, "I can't go hunting with you today"

"What do you mean?"

"Well, this might sound like lame reasoning, but I feel like I need to help someone today"

"Huh?"

"Don't know but I feel strongly compelled to go check out some type of situation at a church."

"Ok then, will I see you tomorrow?"

"Yes"

Immediately Aspot leaves the forest and drives a considerable distance to the church of the ponytailed priest, to help in a totally unknown manner and only because he feels he has been instructed, by the Holy Spirit, to do so. It is now 10 am Saturday morning and nobody is found at any of the church buildings. Aspot waits an hour then shakes his head, thinking that he must have heard wrong. But as he climbs into his jeep and begins to leave a car pulls into the parking lot. He stops to watch a young woman get out of her car and unlock the door of an old church building, then block the main door open. Through the open door he sees her carrying a paint roller and a pan so he approaches her and asks if she needs help.

"Yes!", "I have volunteered to paint this entryway and the descending staircase, into the basement below the tower, but the person who was going to help can't make it." While still talking, she climbs a wobbly scaffold supported by loosely stacked wooden blocks that rest on stairs of different heights. He examines the scaffold and determines that it can be adequately safe if used with extreme caution.

Ascending high, above these steps, are the inner walls of the entry tower a lofty part of the paint job. The scaffold is double height but yet far too short to offer reaching the top of the walls so someone has placed a ladder upon the top scaffold platform which is extended to lean high-up against the wall. As she proceeds to climb this ladder while carrying the pan and roller, he feels a sudden sense of impending danger and quickly scrambles up onto the scaffold to take firm hold of the ladder which is shaking upon the loose rattling scaffold. He asks "Were you really going to try to paint this by yourself?" She responds "Yes."

Aspot shakes his head and watches her paint but it is not long before she is already beginning to lean, too far to the side, to reach a spot too far for her arm's length. Aspot cautions her about the dangers of overreaching from the top of any ladder. And that this ladder is particularly precarious because it is definitely not setting firmly upon solid ground. But she is determined to reach too far into the corner. The scaffold continues to increasingly creak and twist as she leans far towards the left and both ends of the ladder are now certainly trying to move.

With this he calls loudly "Listen, if you keep reaching out like that, I may not be able to hold this ladder. You could be greatly injured or killed if this ladder should suddenly choose to let go. Listen, I am taller, have longer arms and can reach the areas that I am certain you cannot. Please let me paint for a while." With a brush in her hand she straightens, at the top of the ladder to wipe sweat from her brow and says "Ok, I admit that I am scaring myself and there are portions of the wall, especially towards the upper corners that I will really have a hard time reaching".

So, they exchange tasks and as Aspot climbs the ladder and looks down many feet to sharp hard tiled stair edges and a tiled concrete floor, he shudders at the image that comes to mind. Who but only God can know the outcome of that girl had she been allowed to paint that lofty entry without any assistance? To Heaven, Aspot gives thanks for alerting him to help care for this girl, an eager, perhaps reckless, child of God.

The following morning Aspot is back bow hunting again with his brother, in the mountains.

Lightning, Light and Life

As instructed from Heaven, Aspot begins the process of trying to develop a meaningful relationship with the intruder clergyman, in part out of sheer obedience and in part because, for many years, Love (God) has been revealing a bigger issue... 'The Church' and although Aspot is absolutely certain, there is very little he can do, it is out of plain, perhaps morbid, curiosity with what Love has been showing him that causes him to set his face towards the wind and follow God into it.

After numerous futile attempts to establish a reasonable foothold into the environment of the clergyman Aspot is moved in the Spirit and spends a day writing a long letter which directly addresses, in detail, the specific, albeit common, problem of clergy and other men's wives. More specifically there is a certain tradition termed 'Spiritual Fathering" which at times interferes with the role of God fearing family men and is obviously an easy avenue to illicit affairs, especially when privately 'fathering' a wife of an already troubled marriage. The intent of this letter is to highlight the issue in a reasonable manner constructive enough to be shared with and received by clergymen in general.

During this day of letter writing the Spirit is strong and Aspot feels particularly well guided. So that through much prayer and contemplation the content seems accurate, truthful and comfortable enough to feel being meaningfully complete. He has felt strongly moved by God this entire day so now he debates how to close the letter ... he looks up and asks for the proper closure ... but does not hear an answer. It is exceedingly dangerous to end any statement with "As said by God." In this case however, he feels inclined to believe what is written is truly a statement directly from above.

After a short wait for an answer, he begins to debate, with himself and following a, perhaps rashly compelled urge he types "As said by God" ... but then ... exactly as he presses the final period key ... God does answer ... by a bolt of lightning, directly above, that causes an exceedingly close thunder boom which causes every window to rattle very loudly!

This has been a calm day and no storm is in the local atmosphere… "Ah!" Aspot shrieks as he immediately kicks back his chair as his knees and face rapidly find the floor. He is immediately overcome with fear that this closing statement was too far from God's will. But not listening, while still on his knees, straightens back up, quickly deletes the entire letter, empties the trash can, places his face back tightly against the floor and stammers repeated apologies to Heaven

After many minutes of silence he begins to actually listen and hears "Why did you destroy our letter?" "Did you not think that letter, bearing My signature, deserved Me suggesting a better ending punctuation?" … The Holy Spirit is present, caresses Aspot's heart and offers levity.

Amen… Nevertheless, it is immediately understood that this weighted statement from Heaven also carries much other unspoken meaning…

Aspot rewrites the letter but leaves its closure unfinished and does not send it out to anybody… for years. In the meantime God (Love) provides advice, about that letter closure, which covers both sides of the very same coin. While careless 'fathering' is of no small importance to Love (God), so also is our view[s] of God through Life. Let us discuss part of it now.

When we qualify a conviction by claiming "God says" what we are generally only doing is trying to impress others with a type of rather sterile lawful starch. Well, first of all, Love (God) is <u>not</u> sterile! Nor is He starchy. And we should all most certainly know that 'law' is only for strict guidance of those not yet mature enough to understand Love (which obviously includes some, if not many, clergy).

God is Love. 'Love' is both name and noun. We carry Love and Love carries us. Love hopes we might learn to better understand the name so to better carry the noun. Let's make it clear that we are speaking about the one true God, the Father, Son and Holy Spirit. If we are truly walking with God then Love is within us, we within Love and it not necessary to ever say "God says" because it is Love that is speaking through how we reflect/show Love ... This is Life.

A Proverbial Crossroads

Work in Denver has become tedious, life has lost all melody and Aspot's heart refuses to become quiet. He owns a piece of property in the Black Hills and decides it is time to quit his job, move and live there. He discusses his heart and plans with the pastor of the church, in Denver, that he attends. A week later the pastor calls him aside and asks "Would you consider a caretaker's job at a monastery in the Rockies?", "The pay would be very minimal, little more than enough to buy food and fuel, but this change could be a rewarding sojourn for you".

Aspot considers this question. The lifestyle and environment as a caretaker at the monastery in the Rocky Mountains would be little different from living in a cabin in the Black Hills. However, he has worked hard for many years to establish a work history and reputation which has allowed him find software engineering positions in a highly technical arena. Granted, there will be few technical jobs in South Dakota, but he has done some research and knows there is some amount of opportunity for at least an electronic or software technician near his property in the Black Hills.

But the monastery is far from any similar type of side occupation and sits deep in a narrow valley where the ridges on both sides effectively obstruct wireless signals so even a work from home position would be both difficult to establish the needed electrical communication and the type of engineering he specializes in 99% of the time requires being in the lab.

Not wishing to become completely disconnected from technical/engineering work, which he greatly enjoys, he is somewhat sloth in choosing the monastery role because, in part, he still does not have four year college degree in his pocket to bank upon, should he ever feel compelled to go back to the real world.

But then this world seems to offer much heartbreak and other issues. On this note the thought of possibly becoming a monk and the tone of permanence at the monastery is rather appealing. Besides, while in prayer he is reminded of a promise heard from God, many years ago, that still provides him great faith. Furthermore, there is something much bigger in play, he can feel and taste it. In this same regard he also feels the hand of God, is asking to carefully position him ...

Therefore he shortly replies "Yes, I will be the monastery caretaker."

Soon afterward he resigns from his engineering position, loads his jeep and heads towards the southwest rim of the Rocky Mountains, not far from the Santé De Christo mountain range where parishioners are funding the construction of a lofty basilica on the grounds of fledgling monastery. This is a lovely location with approximately 500 acres wrapped on all sides by federally maintained forest and a short hike to the top of the south ridge reveals a grandiose view of majestic Arkansas River canyon. It is an amazingly beautiful part of this country and a wonderful place to find a meaningful measure of peace within an anguishing heart.

The Monastery, the Man and the Mouse

There is an aging two bedroom log cabin reserved for a caretaker and although it has a good roof it has otherwise been poorly cared for. This cabin has numerous holes in the floor and between rooms which has rendered the building rodent infested. Wasting no time Aspot begins to work on the problems of the caretaker's cabin.

During an initial cleanup of the floors, cabinets and closets the well run paths of these rodents are found well pronounced, directly to holes in walls and under fixtures in the kitchen and bathroom. With the traffic so widely proficient it does not seem sensible to set any traps yet. Rather the easiest entries and gross holes are quickly fixed. Within the first week the holes into the walls from the below crawlspace are sealed and the bathroom is completely gutted and all pipe passages securely sealed. New tile is laid starting in the bathroom, then down a short hall and then the kitchen. He decides it is time to start setting traps and initially six standard mouse traps were being simultaneously set every morning, emptied by nightfall and reset for the night.

Within a few days the rate at which multiple mouse traps are being triggered diminishes significantly and so the number of traps is appropriately reduced. Within the two weeks only one trap seems to be necessary. However, this one trap continues to be licked clean of all peanut butter every morning no matter how sensitive it is adjusted to trigger. In fact it is adjusted so sensitive that at times it is almost impossible to set after adding another serving of peanut butter for what seems to one very smart and skilled mouse. A new trap is tried with the same results

After two more weeks of this seemingly fruitless trapping operation he begins to see the humor in this scenario and starts to develop a healthy respect of this critter which manages to continue defying his best attempts at catching it. Nonetheless he is certain that sooner or later that mouse is going to lick the metal tab just a wee-bit too hard and then be just another small bit of unknown history.

This mouse, however, also seems to be becoming rather personable and with a touch of humor because it is increasingly often spotted to be peeking around corners or decidedly watching him from the far end of the short hallway. In not many more days it has become bold enough to remain sitting in open spots, obviously staring with a slight bit of glee as Aspot stares back at it. A type of Russian roulette dialogue between the two seems to be developing and Aspot begins to audibly talk to it by saying things like; "I have every intention of killing you", "Therefore it is in your best interest to find a way out of my home". Meanwhile the mouse rather brashly entertains itself by the thrill of being spotted, twitches it tail and makes barely perceptible squeaks which Aspot perceives to be its way of mocking him with a casual "Hello".

However, one morning, Aspot is sitting on the couch reading and spots that mouse scampering towards him across the carpet. He does not change his position but continues to quietly read and pretend to be paying little attention to that pesky rodent. But when he hears the gentle whisk of its claws climbing the far end of the couch, he tenses slightly with the wild thought of punching it with a clenched fist should it be bold enough to get within his reach.

A smile purses his lips as he hears the mouse begin to scamper towards him across the top of the couch. He pretends not to notice but silently prepares to make a quick move of arm and hand. When it sounds to be getting very close and adrenaline begins to rush, he initiates the swing of his arm and fist. But at the same moment this creature, perhaps sensing his intent accelerates its motion and makes a radically bold motion by literally jumping and landing directly upon Aspot's head. However, also by that time, Aspot's arm is already in an upward swing and so with a quick change of motion opens his hand and successfully cups that mouse under his hand and upon his head. Yes, he has it trapped inside his fist! But "OH, NO!", the thought of it sinking its teeth into his skin suddenly comes to mind and before he can restrain himself his hand reflexively, releases that creature. Of course that mouse immediately jumps from his head and races down the back of that couch quicker than you can say boo!

Oh, so close, yet each of these two creatures, the mouse and the man must have felt some form of victory and defeat at the same time. In fact it does not take but a minute before this mouse is again seen to be galloping across the floor, in plain view, and slide to a stop with a seemingly puffed up boastful pause in the middle of tiled spot in front of the cabin entry door. Aspot imagines it to be gloating and in mouse speak boasting "I trounced the monster and won!" then he laughs and senses the mouse to be laughing along with him.

At this time Aspot says to the mouse "Listen, I actually kind of like you.", "And will hate it when I do finally kill you.", "But I will kill you!", "So if you are sensible, when I open that door right beside you, then you will run out of it and never look back".

Of course Aspot does not think this mouse understands a word of what he saying or that it will allow him to open the front door without racing away, but nonetheless while still speaking Aspot rises from the couch and calmly crosses over to that front door while continuing to talk and with his eyes directly focused upon the mouse. This mouse is also intently watching and greatly surprises Aspot when it does not move as he approaches, because he must appear a giant looming directly above.

However this mouse continues to sit, looking upwards towards him, even while Aspot calmly takes a firm hold of the knob and slowly swings the door open. The mouse continues to watch Aspot carefully; possibly certain it could escape quickly if needed. And as the door swings towards the mouse it also somehow seems to understand and backs up a few steps to allow the door to swing past and wide open.

Then Aspot takes three steps back and says "Now is your chance buddy." At which time the mouse still watching him is imagined to respectfully nod "Goodbye" then turn towards the open door and scamper outside. Aspot quickly closes the door and smiles with a pleasant feeling in heart and wishes this odd friend a grand adventure.

Perhaps that creature, although well fed, had begun to feel isolation from its kind and had taken the chance of finding a friendly 'monster'. In any case, God in the excellence of creation seems to have provided it enough sense in mind to know when to take advantage of an opportunity towards a better life. Aspot goes back to the couch and sits pondering the event with that smile and perhaps feeling even a tiny bit of remorse for the absence of that creature's short friendship. Aspot ponders the simple elegant beauty of the bizarre relationship between him, the mouse, their play and that last moment of shared trust.

But wait … something is jumping up outside the living room window and it looks like a mouse! What is that mouse trying to get back in!? With this thought he runs to the window and looks. There he sees his border collie is, with a loose grip, playfully tossing a mouse, certainly the same one, into the air only to catch and toss it again.

"Hey!"

Running to the door he races out and actually rescues that creature yet still alive although, most certainly, badly bruised. It is panting heavily, probably in pain and definitely terrified! Perhaps it just received an appropriate measure of justice? Aspot discards this thought, mainly because it causes a shudder when also considering the type justice he deserves for behaving human. This poor, bruised creature then gets carefully released under the lattice enclosed deck where it is protected from his playful border collie.

Later, that evening, he finds that his furry friend is gone from where he had sat it. Since then he has often thought of that little guy and every time a smile comes to heart with a hope that it and its family have many comfortable years in a warm barn with a bin full of peanut butter or at least oats☺. However, please trust, that otherwise in general Aspot still greatly dislikes mice and kills every, damage causing, rodent that he can.

6

TEMPERING

Cowboy Fireside Fellowship

Early spring is knocking, the caretaker's cabin is in good shape and Aspot begins ground preparation for assembling a reasonably sized steel frame workshop. This is a building which he had originally purchased for placement on his property in the Black Hills, but after he had offered this building to the monastery committee, for the purpose of storing lawn equipment, it is immediately welcomed with the directive that it be located near the caretaker's cabin.

As fate would have it, about this same time his son, now seventeen, but too long too loosely cared for by both of his parents, loses both his driver's license and his job in account of an alcohol related mishap. Upon hearing his son's recount of the incident, Aspot says "Son, it sounds to me like this would be a good time for you to make a change of course.", "Perhaps come spend time with me in the mountains?"

His son does join his father in the mountains and both get to spend quality time with one another. They get to know each other far in a far better manner than which an 'every other weekend' arrangement from divorce can ever allow. Right out of the chute they begin to develop a much better bonding as they live and lay a foundation to assemble the steel building workshop upon.

Soon, thereafter a local mountain area resident is seen approaching them, in his aging pickup. He has taken notice of the father and son, so has come to introduce himself as David and lets them know that he and his wife can usually be found, any time of the day, just around the closest bend in the canyon, in a log house they have built together. As David starts to get back into his truck he says "Hey, by the way, up past my home by about five miles is a large barn where a number of us are meeting on Saturday evenings to share a community meal, study scriptures and praise the Lord, in a cowboy type of church", "If interested let us know and you can ride along with us", "Ok?"

This offer is well received for various reasons, but possibly the main one being because Aspot's son refuses to travel and attend the church that his father attends on Sunday mornings. But a meal with other people seems to be an acceptable arrangement for his son, even though, he has little interest in what he calls "that conjured-up god, only needed by weak and frightened people"

The following Saturday evening they pile into the back seat David's vehicle and with Aspot's son holding his wife's box containing a delightfully aromatic hot dish, they travel down a well-used jeep trail to an opening in the trees with a tall wooden barn that has new stairs and deck at a door into the upper loft at the east end. The ceiling in the loft is still showing some amount of uncovered new insulation but also fresh pine boards can be seen to being placed, eventually, to cover the entire ceiling.

Approximately twenty residents all living within a ten mile radius show up that night to share a very satisfying pot-luck meal which is then followed by a lovely, worship filled evening. Quickly Aspot considers the moment; and recalls how he had lived in a Denver suburb for years and never knew even the name of his townhome neighbor whose front door was less than six feet from his door. Yet he has been in the mountains for little more than two months and knows the names and shares meals with a majority of the people who live, concealed by forest, for miles all about him. Silently he acknowledges the community found within this rural environment "Wow, how nice!" Almost immediately Aspot's son appears to be truly enjoying these weekly gatherings and after but only a few visits he even warms up enough to begin to join into the bible study portion of the fellowship.

About this same time or within a month of Aspot's arrival another new face also shows, a man only known to have recently moved from Texas. This new man remains quiet and seems to prefer sitting alone, at the far back of the gathering, and silently listen. Everyone listens attentively to the voice of the Baptist minister who weekly travels a considerable distance on Saturdays to preach to this crowd. But winter starts early and the snow gets deep quickly. The long winding gravel road to the cowboy church is becoming far too precarious if not outright treacherous and the Baptist minister asks, the cowboy church, host to be excused from this mission and summarily resigns from the role. This probably shouldn't have surprised anyone, but it did, including the host, who sincerely apologized for the absence of the preacher at the start of that following Saturday fellowship.

It is at this time that the silent man at the back of the room stands up and says, "I can teach, if anyone is interested" All eyes turn back, towards the man in the back, and it is a general consensus of all to hear what the silent man from Texas might have to say. Very quickly everyone realizes that there is something quite different about this Texan who immediately begins to teach with much depth in the meaning of his words. All he has to share seems well worth hearing and closely examining.

In fact it does not take but a few lessons before, Aspot quietly considers the possibility that this new teacher has been destined and positioned by God little different than the manner in which Aspot feels to have been positioned. Of course everyone present is blessed by this new teacher who shares his background history as follows:

The teacher is a married man and a father of two, both graduated from high school. In his youth he had been raised in the Roman Christian faith and had for a short time attended a Roman Catholic seminary but had dropped out to attend a Protestant Christian seminary and eventually became a successful preacher. Time and teaching from both sides of the same coin eventually led to his realization that he was unlikely to ever satisfactorily resolve certain sticky theology issues of not just the Roman Catholic faith but the Protestant Christian camps of theology as well.

He was motivated by truth and began to extensively study materials outside the usual Christian paths which eventually led him to gracefully step down from the pulpit of a now well-established and large Protestant church. This choice was hard but necessary rather than allow his self to preach material he no longer believed to be the full truth. In short, had to stop preaching until, he could know how to teach without knowingly misleading his flock.

Not long after he travelled to Israel and was found deeply intent in the study of a certain scripture by a Jewish rabbi near the West Wall within Jerusalem. The rabbi said "Son I have noticed that you seem focused on some part of that book you hold. Please share with me what it is you study?"

The ex-preacher, said "Rabbi, I am sorry and do not wish to offend you. But this is a Christian bible and I study a scripture that regards the man whom I believe to be the true Messiah."

The rabbi responded, "Son, I have read your book and can understand the concepts your prophet attempts to convey even though I do not align myself with him as the Messiah. Nevertheless, be willing to share the verse which you are so intently studying?"

"This is the book of Mathew from which I read which contains a verse that continues to deeply perplex me. It says '*And from the days of John the Baptist until now the kingdom of heaven suffers violence and the violent takes it by force.*'"

The rabbi laughs and says "You silly Christians, you do not know or understand what you read or preach.", "Your master, Yahshua, was quoting an ancient Jewish commentary", "What he quotes considers one of the prophets in the book, of 'your bible', which you refer to as the 'Old Testament'", "Let me help you understand this quote that you question." At which the rabbi begins to explain in detail the prophecy and the ancient Hebrew commentary which Yahshua quoted from as is recorded within the Gospel according to Mathew.

Although there remained a definite difference in opinion about Yahshua (Jesus) being the Messiah, this encounter was the beginning of a long-lasting friendship between this man and the rabbi. It is understood that this Texan teacher is diligent on a search for Truth so we will call him Truth Seeker (TS). TS continued to reside in Israel, for more than a year, often studying under that same rabbi but remaining faithful to Yahshua or who we most often call Jesus. Upon returning back to America TS got a job as a grade school teacher which is where he met and married his wife.

Meanwhile TS continued to look up and listen to the Spirit and one day he was moved by the Spirit to construct a large wooden cross and go stand on the lawn in front of the capital of Texas because he believed he had been told "While you stand with Me on the lawn no idol will stand atop the Texas capitol building"

You see, it was expected by Texas residents that on a certain day of May, that year, a new statue of, an idol, the "Goddess of Liberty" was to be mounted atop the dome of the newly refurbished capitol building. However, as directed, by the Spirit, TS built a wooden cross fourteen feet in height. Then every day for fourteen days he diligently carried it early onto the lawn in front of the capital building and held it upright during normal contractor work hours of each of the fourteen days. When the construction workers left for the day so did he.

During, this time news reports that between May 31 and June 14, 1986 over 50 attempts were made, to set the new 'Goddess of Liberty' upon its mount atop the dome. Each time regardless of the effort made it looked as if the feet of the idol would dance, like the end of a magnet dances with another magnet of the same polarity, about the top of the dome. Local news media takes notice of TS and asks why he is holding the very large cross in front of the capital building. He answers "Because 'I Am' told me to be here", "And as long as this cross is here that goddess idol will not set a foot atop the dome of the capitol building".

Indeed for fourteen days he is on that lawn and for fourteen days no amount of effort can get that idol to set down on the dome mount (See Goddess References). However at the end of the fourteenth day, he hears the Holy Spirit again and is told to no longer be present at the capital. The Spirit lets him know that the Lord's statement and point has been accomplished and his mission has been successful. That day, TS does not go with the cross to the lawn and on June 14, the idol called the goddess of liberty, was effortlessly set down upon the dome the first try.

Years later this man, still a school teacher, listening to the Spirit hears "Move to the mountains". This perplexed him because he was not in any financial position to afford an arbitrary, sudden move to anywhere. Yet he continued to hear the same message and trusting the wisdom of the Holy Spirit, TS and wife quit their jobs, packed up their family and bought an empty mountain lot, they could afford, in the southern Rockies positioned amongst and above trees with a clear view directly toward the east. Soon he hears about a tall wooden barn that is, in part, being used for a Christian fellowship meeting place, southward along the top of same ridge. And now, you know how the teacher, TS, really, long earlier, first entered the story.

Goddess References:

1. The Victoria Advocate, Wednesday, June 11 and 15, 1986, article titled "To Put Goddess on Dome Texas Guard Calls for Help"

2. The Bulletin, Wednesday, June 11 and 15, 1986, article titled "Putting goddess back on capital a Texas-size task"

As the knowledge of the new teacher became slowly revealed the nature of the Cowboy Church begin to change in an appropriate manner and this fellowship is truly become a blessed part of Life for Aspot and his son. There is always much food, study, dancing, singing, meditation and growth. It is worthy to note, that although Aspot truly enjoying the incredible time of fellowship he still continues to make a two hundred mile, round trip journey to the closet church, of his faith, on Sunday mornings because he continues to desire the blessing which accompanies Holy Communion.

Now TS, is well aware of the manner in which human nature possesses an inclination towards becoming overly zealous about any seemingly, exciting new view of God and he starts early to periodically warn everyone about running new concepts too far off track. This is because he believes that excessive interest in some threads of what he is going to teach that might seem new can too easily result in someone trying to yet again start another cult. Repeatedly, TS reminds everyone to understand how important it is to remember that we are all members of the one 'Church' of which Yahshua is the head.

Furthermore, he stresses the importance of <u>not</u> getting wrapped up in Messianic Jewish theology which has some heretical elements that need to be avoided. In general, he tries hard to maintain a straight heading keel towards Life while yet introducing new angles of looking at scripture and Yahshua that are not typically considered these days by most Christian religions. Overall the Saturday Cowboy Fellowship seems well aligned and augments the common Christian faith.

An overview of this new content within the Cowboy Fellowship lessons is heavily focused upon the society which Jesus (Yahshua) grew up within, the angle at which his disciples would have likely seen Him is described as having been commonly taught and understood by all who walked with Him to such a degree, that the early writers might not of thought it necessary to mention these things. In short what was potentially possible for everyone, at the time Yahshua (Jesus) was born, the environment He quite likely grew as a boy within and would have inherently understood what it means to be a "perfected man". This is important because Scriptures instructs us "be perfect just as your Father in Heaven is perfect" and this is important because Love came to this earth as a 'son of man' to show us how every son of man can learn, try to emulate and walk with Him.

TS, never seems offended by critical questions and one day when Aspot challenged a topic taught, TS said "You honor me by testing the integrity of my lessons" and then successfully continued to explain in great detail the reason to believe the truth of that lesson. Upon this note Aspot silently thanks God for providing a good teacher. It seems to be a purposed step, one of the many, to those that had already proceeded and others to follow. Life dancing with Love is 'Good'!

Caretaker's Garden

Daily as the sun pokes its first rays over the top of the east canyon rim Aspot climbs a steep rocky knoll with a green hardbound psalter in hand. At the top of this knoll and at the top of his voice he sings the morning song (Psalms) assigned for that day. Then while descending back down, with a few tools kept present, he continues to shape an ever improving pathway between valley bottom and the large granite boulders atop the ridge, where he joyfully sings the Psalms. This small task is a small pleasant chore and a desire of heart.

The next task of the day is to attend a garden that had only been recently established with the help of a friend, tractor and plow that carved open a reasonable sized plot in dark, rich soil of the meadow. This garden is near a gurgling creek from which the garden water is sourced. A fence is built about the garden making it difficult for deer to easily tread the various common vegetables that have now been planted. And the garden grows.

The many other tasks would then commence, such as mending much fallen fence, clearing the monastery forest of a pine beetle infestation, by dropping and delimbing trees. Then stacking the logs in piles and covering with a black (roll) plastic cover which when sealed with dirt at the bottom created a solar oven which baked the trees and killed the beetles. There is much of this type of work. There are also lawns to be mowed, newly planted trees to be watered and many other typical maintenance duties. Aspot's son helps in many of these tasks and overall, it is an enjoyable father/son service for God and brothers of Spirit.

Then as the sun begin to descend across the tree line to the west, Aspot again treads the path up the steep knoll with the psalter in hand and joyfully sings the evening song of that day. Lastly he cooks dinner for his son and himself.

One day as the glow of the sun and Santa De Christo mountain tops in the west helped paint a lovely evening setting as they finish their tasks and stand discussing in front of a skid loader which at this time is fitted with a flat vertical blade, for road maintenance. They are facing the widest part of the meadow and the setting sun. As though out of nowhere, a rock, about three inches in diameter, whistles past, between them and strikes the vertical blade causing a loud "wham!" that echoes down the canyon. Instantly both heads turn towards the cause of the loud bang and quickly notice the rock shattered at the base of the blade. It is immediately obvious that someone must have just thrown this rock directly at them and so startled they both with a yell scanned the perimeter from which this rock has come trying to see who has just attacked them. But all they can see is a wide peaceful grass filled meadow of which they know a brook is gently gurgling at some distance from them.

After much dialogue as to what could have caused this rock to happen, it is decided that because of both the angle it came from and the fact that the pieces of the rock are cool that it did not come from the upper atmosphere but rather had to have been cast by something from directly in front of them. But the direction they must look has only but short grass and there is nobody or any observable creature present. They gather the pieces, of the shattered rock, and find that all the large pieces fit tightly back together into a rock about three inches in diameter.

So, this event is considered an interesting supernatural mystery by Aspot. But because his son does not believe in anything spiritual or supernatural for him it is only a rather disturbing yet what must certainly be scientifically explainable phenomena. Nevertheless, we can be sure that now the son is beginning to re-evaluate what he chooses to believe because he later discusses the rock event with the neighbor David who although also perplexed by the story offers a possible solution.

Apparently an entire Native American tribe has been massacred in that meadow a hundred years, or so, earlier.

In fact the Tallahassee creek is named after the chief of that tribe. David suggests the possibility that many Native American spirits might remain not properly put to rest and are protesting the intrusion of their meadow. Within a week, the Orthodox Rite of Passage is performed over the meadow and who knows the whole story, but no further activity of similar phenomena is known to have since occurred at that location.

The garden continues to grow with the many tomato plants becoming quite large with much fruit developing. However, the source water from the creek is first obtained by an aged wooden sleuth that feeds an old irrigation ditch is diverted to the garden. But because it is a dry summer the creek level drops below the point where water can no longer be collected in this manner. Therefore, Aspot resorts to building a small dam in the creek near the garden and carrying pails of water dipped out of that dam to the many green vegetable plants which continue to happily grow and produce crops.

However, this summer continues without any noticeable rain and the flow of the creek eventually comes to a complete stop and bed dries up so that the water hole behind the creek damn becomes little more than a small puddle of water. Aspot has seen the problem coming but has also continued to hope for the rain which has not appeared. So finally, one morning, he must resort to using two buckets in order to even partially fill one bucket with water, by dipping out small amounts of water with one bucket to slowly fill the other. Then he carries this one bucket of water and sparingly applies it to the tomato plants, which need it the most.

There is very little muddy moisture remaining in the water hole as he starts walking back to the cabin. But as

105

he walks he hears "Where are you going?" At which Aspot responds "Lord, I am going to the cabin" The Spirit asks "Why?" Aspot responds "Because my garden needs water and the water hole is dry" The Spirit then asks "Is that water hole really dry?" Aspot can only answer "Well, no but there is very little water left at best." At which the Spirit questions him with "Are you sure?"

This dialogue seems a bit odd even to Aspot who trusts in the voice of the Spirit, because it is obvious that water hole is all but totally bone dry. But knowing that the Holy Spirit would not taunt him in such a way over a dead horse, he chides himself for probably only having a stupid discussion with himself and continues to walk. However he hears again "Where are you going?" Aspot stops walking and listens to hear "Do not believe that your little is too little" The Spirit then also immediately adds "To those who can see the little as being great, more will be received. But to whom the much is considered too little all will be lost" Upon hearing this Aspot turns around to go back and worry out even the smallest bit of moisture from that water hole that he can"

He gets on his knees and begins to dip small amounts in the one bucket and empty in the second. After some amount of effort he does again fill get a full bucket of brown water and there is yet a very small amount of water remaining. So after he carefully distributes this bucket of water he goes back to the water hole to get every last bit he can. But when he arrives back at the water hole he can see that it is now a bit fuller than earlier and so he now easily fills a bucket.

Again he returns after spreading the water but this time finds the water hole now has enough water in it to easily fill both buckets with clean water. Upon return again the water hole is now way over half full. Aspot is overcome with a mixture of intense emotion that knows without doubt that is was truly God with whom he had been dialoguing. He continues to carry water to that garden and the pond fills to the brim, but does not run over. As he continues to water he is now singing songs of praise and thanksgiving and the plants are soon watered better than ever before.

"Oh, thank you Lord!" "Thank you, thank you and thank you!" As he now walks back to the cabin he continues to thank God. But then he stumbles and says "Please forgive me Lord, but my faith is too small to expect your help again this way tomorrow" At which he hears "Why did you say that?!" Aspot now embarrassed ponders his spurious doubt of faith and seeks for an answer to give the Holy Spirit. However before he has an answer he hears "It does not matter because you have now already declared the outcome of tomorrow."

The following morning that water hole is indeed bone dry that much water was lost … but not the additional new measure of faith and wisdom he has been granted …

Not many days later, while on his knees within the garden the Holy Spirit reminds him of a vision and Aspot knows it is nearing his time to return to the real world …

Time to Reencounter the Dragons

His son has joined a military service and is now at boot-camp training. The monastery build-up is taking off slower than expected and with much of the initial caretaker type of work complete, the garden finished for the season and the financial reserve in his bank account about depleted Aspot wakes one morning and feels in the spirit that it is time to start searching for a job and prays audibly to God "Lord, I sense that it is time for me to go back into the world of dragons. Please help me find a job."

For half an hour Aspot then sits quietly reading scripture and ponders just what kind of work a man, without a college degree, who has been out of the work force for a year and a half and who has limited access to the job market might hope to find. What types of jobs should he apply and how to find them. These questions he has known he would someday need to resolve but he has not really considered them until this moment.

The phone rings and upon answering hears "Aspot, I know that we have hardly met, it has been a long time since we have talked and this call might not be important. But I feel that I should call you this morning to let you know about an open engineering position that you might be interested in."

The man who called is a contract engineer whom Aspot has only met once in that man's home which had showed much evidence to be a Godly family. This phone call came from totally out of the blue and completely unexpected. Aspot calls this company immediately and by 4:00 pm that same day, Aspot has been formally offered and accepted an engineering position that only his dreams could hope for.

Because Aspot has not sent out resumes, applied for any other employment or in any fashion besides a prayer to God half an hour earlier let anyone know he needed a job since coming to the caretaker's cabin he is convinced that God provided him this one. How else but God? Praise the LORD!!!

This also seems a good time to inject something further. Many years earlier while still in Washington State, (The time in the furnace) he was attending college but when selecting the courses to take the following semester the Holy Spirit asks him "What are you doing?" of which he responds "I am choosing my next semester college courses". The Spirit asked "Why?"

Aspot felt a nudge with that question and with raised eyebrows replied "Because I a need college degree." But he is caused to pause when the Holy Spirit says "You are worth more to me if you do <u>not</u> get that degree you seek". Aspot, trusting the voice of the Holy Spirit, summarily stopped attending college at that time in his life. However from that time forward he continued becoming increasingly proficient and successful in an engineering field without a four year degree. He remains certain to this day that he never needed to fear lacking what he needs. Faith is a wonderful gift. Obedience is rewarded with strength and greater resolve towards good. Love walks seamlessly with both! Perfection comes by observing all three equally. None appreciate vanity … Let us do our best, despite, at times, being a little too human …

Back in the World

Aspot is now back working an eight hour shift like everyone else and life is good. He is renting an apartment with a pool and his granddaughter comes to visit every so often and swims in the community pool. Work is exciting, challenging and rewarding.

Vern

With trepidation Aspot assumes a task of leading an adult bible study in an elderly people home following a request from, someone he has developed much respect of in recent months, a friend over-extended, leading bible studies in multiple elderly care homes and certainly needing help. The elderly home appears to be a state sponsored facility, very basic, understaffed and although relatively clean, has a pervasive lingering odor of rancid urine present throughout every niche of its long buffered hallways.

Aspot soon becomes somewhat familiar with the people in this elderly home, the care givers, the many whom lived there both those that attended the bible study and those who chose not. The attendance to this weekly bible study is small in proportion to the number of residents although, it is easy to develop conversation with everyone who lives here through open bedroom doors following a warm hello.

It should be said that working with the elderly is a noble task regardless of the role of those who do the work. But, more importantly, just as valuable are the workers for the elders, are the elders for the workers and all visitors especially the young people. You see, the aged persons truly do possess vast reserves of overly hidden wisdom captured in their minds and hearts. Men and women who have long worked, struggled, learned, played, shared and still, most certainly, know how to show love. The hearts of elders, supposed to be near the finish line, can be better viewed as an opportunity for sharing the reward of their race well run. Some of the most golden stories can be foundational lessons spoken through few, if any, words.

The bible study participants met Wednesday nights, in the community cafeteria mostly by their own efforts often by use of a walker or wheelchair. As Aspot is introduced to the elders he is asked to lead a bible study with it is made known that there are three regularly attending individuals who generally need some amount of personal assistance that sometimes comes from the help of a trained aid, but more often the help of the person leading the bible study.

One of these is a man named Vern observed to quietly sit with a pronounced slouch and sidewise lean within a wheelchair during fellowship. So with these things made known it is apparent that Aspot must arrive early enough to adequately assist every elder willing to attend.

The first day Aspot is solely expected to lead, he arrives fifteen minutes early to help the regular bible study attendees and others who might ask. At his arrival he was met at the door by Martin who is in his seventies, in good health, carrying his bible and always ready to help get the bible study going. Martin and Aspot walked the halls, offering reminders and determining who needed help getting to the bible study. Aspot is eager to see many persons attend the bible study, but is not prepared for Vern.

Vern must have been in his nineties and it seems to have lived a very full life, still loves his long departed wife but now very weak, wheelchair bound and a greatly failing memory. This first night he finds Vern sitting in a wheelchair within his room. Aspot remembers his name and greets him. Vern, moving little asks "Who are you?" Aspot informs Vern that he is going to be leading their weekly bible-study for some unforeseeable amount of time. Vern acknowledges his intent to attend the bible study with a strong and simple "Yes." But then mentions that he needs to use the toilet first".

Aspot responds "Ok, I will go find one of the aids to help you" and then spends most of his early arrival time searching for an aid willing to help Vern use the toilet. He finally does locate an aid who offers to help in a moment and who also promises to then also take Vern to the bible study.

It was nearly fellowship start time, with all expected to attend gathering closely around tables in the cafeteria, except for Vern. Aspot goes to check on Vern while Martin continues to help everyone else get seated and distribute song books. However, upon return to Vern's room it is with a bit of surprise to Aspot that he is again greeted by this question "Who are you?"

This only indicates that Vern's short term memory is greatly diminished. However the fact that Vern has not yet used the toilet and is now asking him for help causes Aspot to blush and stammer "Oh, I am not qualified to help you with that" and is spared at this moment by the convenient appearance of the aid he had talked to earlier. With a smile Aspot tells Vern "Your help is here, I will see you in the cafeteria shortly" and quickly returns to the group.

"Hi there everyone!", "Sorry I am late", "Lets sing a couple songs", "Martin what do you suggest we start with?" "Page seventeen", and although still missing Vern, all others attendees chime into the best possible harmony and sing "♪Rock of ages ...♪"

Finally well into the bible study, not seeing Vern arrive, the lead excuses self to go find out why. Then even at a distance Vern could be seen still sitting in exactly the same spot as earlier. So quickly bypassing Vern's door, he searched for someone to attend to Vern's needs and meets a nurse in the hallway. She smiles, acknowledges the situation and promises to assist Vern. Aspot returns to the bible-study and does not to see Vern show up until nearly the end of the allotted bible study period. So he makes a mental note to arrive much earlier the following week so that he could make sure Vern can attend the bible-study as Vern wishes.

The following week Aspot arrives at Vern's room a half hour before the bible-study is to start, and is not surprised to be asked "Who are you?" Aspot smiles, confirms that Vern needs help in the bathroom and asks someone at the front desk where he can find an aid or nurse. Then he walks the hallways looking for help and encounters two staff members who both promise to help Vern when they can. Meanwhile Aspot continues to walk the halls and invite residents to attend the bible-study. The bible-study start time is near so Aspot goes to check on Vern but finds him still unmoved and again because Vern does not remember who Aspot is and thinks him to be an aid asks for help in the bathroom. Aspot again loudly declares "I am not qualified to help you in the bathroom". Then he quickly goes back to the front desk, explicitly requests a health care assistant's help with Vern and goes to the bible study. Vern does not show up at the bible study at all this evening.

The next week he again shows up early and at Vern's room but this time finds Vern sitting upon his toilet and immediately hears "Help me." Aspot responds, "Hold on a moment, I will be right back". It seems all of the staff must have been abducted by alien space rays because not a one can be found except the receptionist at the front desk who can be seen to roll her glazed eyes. Ok, perhaps care of the elderly is not considered a noble task by the front desk receptionist?

Not knowing what to do but certain that he promised Vern that he would return soon Aspot scrambles back to Vern's room where Vern is found still sitting on the toilet. Vern says "I need help" but when Aspot stands in pause, Vern asks "Who are you?" Aspot although very certain that he is in a precarious situation, finally takes notice, feels Love whisper and verbally repeats what he just heard "I am someone who is here to help you" And for the first time in his life takes off his jacket and hat to wipe an innocent old man's butt and put a new diaper on an innocently aged man.

Vern attended bible-study, on time this evening and every week forward because although the very personal duty of helping an aged man with toilet needs never became an easy challenge, he continues to assist Vern as needed, which included, at times, brushing Vern's false teeth and so forth. Perhaps only now is Aspot beginning to develop shape and becoming qualified for the task of leading a bible study.

Yet the better lesson soon follows. Vern always shows eagerness to attend the bible-study. Even though it seems he remembers little he always remains aware of the day and time bible-study is to start. Then when arriving at the bible-study, innocent in spirit and simple like a child, seemingly nearly void of a memory, eyes closed he appears to be quietly napping while others discuss the scripture or scriptural topic of the day. Aspot honestly does not think Vern is getting anything out of the study. Then one day, when the room becomes quiet for a few moments during the discussion, Vern not moving from his usual posture of a leaning slouch against the rail of his wheel-chair, as if waking from a deep sleep, slowly with astonishing clarity, using few words, expounds the deeper meaning of the verse being discussed.

The depth of insight Vern showed greatly surprised Aspot who also marveled and pondered what he had just heard. Vern had just presented a significant but gently subtle point about that verse, a gift of deeper understanding and knowledge. From that day on Vern could be counted on to offer similar insight into whatever the spiritual discussion of the week might be. Having noted the need to make room for Vern to speak, purposely Aspot would pause and present moments of silence that asked for and allowed time for whatever treasure Vern might have to offer. Everyone was only ever disappointed when Vern should choose to remain quiet.

The manner in which Aspot had arrogantly considered Vern to be little more than a man returned to childhood, an ancient relic with little to offer, was a for Aspot, reason to feel shame and embarrassment. However more importantly, Vern, the man child of God, is an example that should greatly encourage us to hope for the kind of deeper wisdom that follows having God (Love) ever present in our Life. Even if we should lose our short-term memory and bodily strength, the God which, in our daily life, we earnestly search for, accept and allow residing within, can ever be trusted to never lose luster. Life of God never grows weary, decays or grows too old!

A little over a year later, it came as little surprise to find Vern's room in the elder care center totally empty with only clean sheets and a blanket upon what had once been his bed. A query of the front desk only confirmed the answer that Aspot expected. Every bit of Vern and his life has vanished with the blink of an eye.

The bible study this evening is somber, not only because of Vern's absence, but because some weeks earlier Aspot had taken employment in Denver which is sixty miles north and getting to the bible study after work on time is become a difficult scramble. Besides, winter is setting in and the snow is not helping. Aspot has been trying to decide how he can continue to spend time with these wonderful people and still enjoy the effort. The passing of Vern has helped him decide to let everyone know that he will not come back the following week but will miss seeing all of them.

7

TUNING THE EDGE

Mid-Winter Blossoms

Oh, the hoary-frost that makes crystal sculptures of every tree! We are so very blessed to be positioned in the middle of such wonderful artwork of God. Oh the beauty of the light amidst the snow! It is the middle of December and winter has most definitely already announced its arrival. Yet, Aspot gets up daily well before the sun begins to rise, so that he might miss most commuter traffic and this generally causes him to miss the manner in which early sunshine dances upon the snow. It is no different today as he makes a pot of coffee, drinks a cup and pours the remainder into a thermos. It is gently snowing outside as he starts the car and lets it warm while removing a couple inches of new snow off the vehicles windows.

He slides into the seat, lets his glasses clear a moment and then his eyes focus on a bush being highlighted by the headlights...what he sees makes him immediately get back out of the car and examine this bush. What a

116

surprise! It is covered with lively green leaves, bright yellow blossoms and a slight layer of snow! This bush is one of nearly a hundred that surround his lawn and all of them months ago had lost the last of their leaves for the winter. All the rest remain leafless … but this one is clothed in its cheerful green leaf spring attire and adorned with colorful blossoms … how is this possible?!

Only Love knows the answer, yet for no defendable reason, Aspot immediately pictures Vern which has left a lingering association of Vern with this mysterious bush being awakened to Life in the middle of winter while everyone else sleeps. Who knows but God?

The Chalice

Winter continues and early every Saturday morning Aspot joins a group of devoted people who peacefully gather to receive Holy Communion and say the Rosary (a prayer, since his earliest memory has been recited daily by his parents and much of his family) on a sidewalk across the street from an abortion clinic. It is not unusual for it to be excessively cold in these very early hours but without missing a beat the hearts of this group regularly join in spirit with the most innocent and helpless this day of the week to pray for all Life in the womb, at risk of losing their heart beat, might be spared.

The outcome of these prayers is generally unknown but this morning a car stops alongside them and a young woman gets out and introduces herself. She lets them know that she is on her way to work but has long wanted to let them know that she has a happy baby at home that is only alive because she had seen this group the morning she was scheduled to have an abortion but was moved that day in heart and did not go into the clinic. She just wanted everyone to know that she and her baby are eternally grateful for their continuing devoted effort. Likewise this group is thankful for her offering this blessing to them and Life.

It is now Spring/Summer and one Friday afternoon, Aspot just home from work, takes notice of a peculiar, distinctly shaped, it seems, cloud sitting alone in the wide blue sky. It shows an image that is so well defined that it immediately catches his undivided attention and he leans against his car, watches and waiting for it to disburse, as all clouds and jet steam marks do. However, after many minutes he sees no hint that this cloud is losing any detail of its distinct shape. .

This cloud looks like a wine glass (chalice) very similar to the shape one might see being used during Holy Communion, but outlined with what looks to be flames wrapping about the stem and proceeding upwards past the top of cup. He has been watching this sight for over half an hour now and it remains perfectly very well defined and so he is beginning to doubt it is a cloud or jet mark but some other phenomena.

It has now been over an hour and this image in the sky has not changed its shape or definition but is moving away, it seems the speed of which this earth rotates. He runs to find a camera and capture an image of it before it gets much smaller. By this time it is quite some distance from him and appears located directly above Pikes Peak which is about forty miles to the southwest of him. From this apparent location of the object in the sky he estimates it to be about the same size as the mountain over which it is suspended. Eventually the glow from this well-defined image of a chalice disappears over the horizon.

The next morning, Aspot is with the usual group participating in the church service across the street from an abortion clinic. As the priest recites the liturgy of faith in mass service and lifts up with both hands a chalice which contains wine spiritually transformed, into the blood of a man hanging on a cross, and the angle at which Aspot watches, this chalice rises above Pikes Peak. With much glisten this metallic cup reflects the rosy rays of early morning, from its surface as if fire is wrapping about the stem, upward past its rim. He watches this chalice claim a portion of his view the same as the mountain in the background. He is immediately moved to believe that, at this moment, he is revisiting a tangible version of a vision he has experienced the previous evening and holds in greater faith, the fact, this cup contains quite humbly, immense power; the very Blood of Christ.

Rain and Canyon

Our Life is provided with two realms. One is visible, tangible and we can touch it. The other is invisible, mysterious but yet touches us. The visible realm is provided so that we might learn from the manner of which can observe creation to behave before and after our touch. Over time (generations) the knowledge we have learned from creation is shared by hearing advice from our parents whom have either suffered or been pleased from experiences they have obtained. We call this accumulated and shared knowledge, as appropriate, either common sense or natural law. This is a story about both ...

It is the end of another work week and Aspot heads south from Denver towards an old mining community in the mountains. As he leaves the interstate at Colorado Springs and begins to head towards the mountains on Highway 24 it begins to lightly rain. By the time he is mile into the canyon, that Highway 24 snakes, divided by the creek, along near the bottom of, rain is coming down hard, very hard. In fact it seems the sky is opened and a sea is descending upon travelers. It has become difficult to see the road and 'common sense' thoughts, of caution, begin to flash in his mind.

This road is very winding and this canyon bottom is going to be very tight for about another five miles and already water is beginning to flow like a stream on the outside lane tightest to the canyon wall by the sloping manner in which the this entire road seems to have been purposely constructed and all vehicles begin immediately to migrate into the higher (passing) lane. This is not only to avoid the small stream, of rain water, in the other lane but to also missing hitting many small rocks that are also already washing into that lane. Traffic comes to a barely even a crawl but common sense is now yelling "Get out of here!"

Aspot evaluates the situation; traffic is moving at less than two miles an hour, but the rate of which rain is falling, is itself predicting a disaster unless traffic starts moving much faster. This does not seem likely and there is no way to move faster unless he is willing to brave the stream of water and the many small rocks moving within the lower lane. His car is a small two door sedan, which sits low and, in the past, he has had to replace the oil pan after hitting a road construction bump too hard. But the potential of a canyon flood overwhelms his concern for this car being damaged.

Little more than two seconds later, he pulls back into the lower lane and accelerates. Yes, he is hitting many small rocks and water is splashing like crazy under the chassis, and soon contending the deepening water and increasingly larger rocks. In not long his front grill begins to push the stream and the splashing across his windshield even with wipers moving fast provide less than the needed road visibility and his car bounces crazily from the rocks being hit.

In the passing lane, on the left of his car, is a long, bumper to bumper, line of, it seems, all other vehicles that also seem to have come to a complete stop. But now with a whitened knuckle grip he steers like a madman, testing the integrity of his engine, drive train and tires while driving into the mouth of increasingly adverse conditions. Yet he makes it to where the canyon opens out into a wide mountain valley where the flow of water is changed and running like a wide shallow river perpendicularly across both lanes little more than about four inches deep. He observes that the car leading everyone in in the passing lane is sitting atop a slight knoll, totally free of any water but completely stopped, as if afraid to cross even this relatively shallow water ahead of it. Does that driver not know that he is effectively trapping every person, in a long line of cars winding down the narrow canyon behind him? And he wonders, why does no one else pull out to pass the car in the lead?

Aspot's face is also white from the tension of the moment and with worries that his engine might yet stall, with little more thought he keeps moving. Approximately thirty minutes later, he is greeted by friends whom have been waiting and praying for him. They have been worried about his safety because they have been watching the local TV station, that is already broadcasting live and showing cars, hitting buildings as they are washed by torrential waters, out the bottom of the canyon. Persons, observed being swept away in the rampaging current, as they try to escape trapped autos, are being reported.

Aspot gives a sincere "thank you" to God and joins into the prayers of his friends for the people missing and still trapped within the canyon wide river but speaks little about his journey. Rather he, quietly, feels shame for having escaped a disaster while others are even now still perishing. Had he not observed, an entire train of cars stopped, by the leading auto, perhaps only from fear of rather shallow water, at the valley entrance? Perhaps that driver simply didn't have the 'where to' (sense) to consider the danger imposed upon those trapped in the canyon behind him?

Silently Aspot, rebukes himself and asks why he had not made some attempt to get that lead car driver to either move forward or out of the way, so that those behind might escape … He failed to make any attempt to save life when he might have only needed to have spoken a few words of common sense into the ears of another man…an error … a defenseless omission … and perhaps rust deepens within an increasingly soundless lock …

With this thought the tone of this book must deepen … perhaps more careful … mindful of what Love has been teaching …

Granddaughter's Great Demise

Follows is an experience, that actually occurred some years earlier, and a type of high water mark for how we fail to hear, understand or possibly even raise a 'high fist' against God. Of all the many Spiritual lessons, Aspot has encountered, this one, although not to him most personally painful, is yet the most somber and weighted by much interest from God. It is, to Love (God) a certain very bad taste … Listen people, because hearing is far better than being broadsided by "the slow train" most certainly approaching.

Aspot's daughter and granddaughter move into Aspot's home so that she can attend a local vocational school. He is delighted by the delightful presence of both of these daughters. And it so happens that at this time his granddaughter is at an age appropriate, for the faith, yet of her mother, to receive what some churches refer to as 'First Communion'. Aspot volunteers to help make sure his granddaughter gets to the required weekly (preparatory) training. He first suggests that she receive 'Chrismation' and 'First Communion' in the Orthodox Catholic faith he attends rather than the Roman Catholic Church but his daughter adamantly demands that her daughter receives First Communion in a Roman Catholic Church.

Please allow this chapter to be a bit technical because it is going to address a fuzzy topic about the two largest and, perhaps, most confused groups of Christians, who are the Roman and Orthodox Catholics. These two streams of faith are distinctly and explicitly divided religions even though both started out 'the same faith'. No good deed goes without finding attention from Ha'satan, thereby religious politics took a firm foothold and by the thirteenth century 'division' had become fully completed with a footprint called "The Great Schism".

However, pride does not consider any horse dead until it has kicked, dissected and mauled it into a messy puddle. Between these two parties the kicking has continued. However Aspot's granddaughter, now eight years old, has often attended both Orthodox and Roman Catholic churches and is reasonably curious, about the difference between the two, which, as best she can tell, seem to be the same church. So she asks her grandfather to explain the difference.

He lets out a deep sigh, because the main differences, in their theologies, are small, subtle, based upon egos trying to describe 'the wind'. The real issue is pride. When putting the politics aside, the split (division) of the "Universal Church" is simple and so he describes the difference between the two 'Catholic' faiths by using a childish fairytale which can be pondered by a young girl as follows:

The Brawling Brothers

Once upon a time a great king gifted all of his loyal people with a beautiful garden full of delicious fruits, lawns and play areas which occupy an island, the king's home, close to the main land where the people of his kingdom live. For access to his gift he also provides a sturdy bridge. This king is kind and understands how the efforts and toils, of his people, are arduous and can cause them to lose their smile should they not regularly rest and enjoy Life. Yes the people of his entire kingdom are important enough to him that he considers all of them as being a part of his own family. And it pleases the king to watch his family, often spend time away from their daily tasks visiting and resting in his garden. His people love their king. They greatly appreciate how he treats them as his own family and therefore together as one, his kingdom is joyful and very productive.

Now preparing for a long journey he assigns a certain young family to be the trusted caretakers of the bridge to his garden. His garden requires no maintenance for it has been created as perfect as his love which can be easily seen ever present within it. Then the king leaves to visit a far country. His kingdom family misses seeing their king and papa, yet they remain happy and feel safe especially while within his garden.

The king is patient about returning and remains distant for many seasons. Meanwhile the bridge caretaker family has two brothers, Ortho`s and Roma and they tend their assigned family responsibilities, do their duties well and often enjoy assisting other kingdom family members across the bridge so that everyone might continue to joyfully find delight with the king's glorious garden. Eventually however the son, named Roma begins to feel more competent than his brother and desires to be solely in charge of the bridge and its maintenance and begins to push his brother. Ortho`s also has an ego and pushes back. Soon the pushing turns into much shove.

Their vain interests eventually became an outright brawl which spreads across the entire width in the middle of the bridge. The other families are at first only shocked by this awkward situation and wait patiently for the two caretaker brothers to settle their dispute. However the brawl continues and the people become exceedingly sad because the intense enmity of struggle on the bridge is blocking their passage to and from the garden. But also the struggle for control of the bridge is causing anyone attempting to get past the angry brothers being badly bruised from wayward blows. And beyond this, often those attempting to get past the foray are at times even yanked into the scuffle and injured enough to die.

As time goes past the people and their families, stop going to the garden because it is become just too dangerous. But mostly because their memory is frail and they forget about the beauty, fruit, joy and rest in the garden. Over time the entire kingdom becomes quite unhappy and unproductive. Even worse the kingdom becomes wicked. People become hateful towards each other and 'good' becomes unknown. Families become sick and broken. Children are being sacrificed for pleasure. Men are sleeping with other men. And many forms of every type of evil begin to greatly abound. Yes even on the bridge! But the brothers continue to brawl and take little interest in the people unless they happen to venture too near to the scuffle. In general the caretaker family seems to have totally lost all concern for family, the garden, the bridge and their king.

Aspot stops the tale at this point and the granddaughter says "I do not think this story ended" and she asks "What happens when the king returns?"

Taste and See

His granddaughter begins the weekly lessons, at the Roman Catholic Church, to prepare, for receiving her first Holy Communion, which is a series of weekly classes that will take months. Meanwhile he also makes sure that she attends the late Sunday Roman Catholic church services; even though he personally also attends an Orthodox Catholic Church service. His granddaughter is filled with excitement in regards to receiving her first communion and repeatedly lets him know that she is eager to "eat the bread".

Approximately half way through the First Communion lesson series the Roman parish education director approaches Aspot and tells him that he must register in their parish. Aspot at that time responds that he was a very active member of another Catholic faith and that his granddaughter is herself registered in this parish and attending Sunday morning services. It seems the education director is satisfied, because she says nothing further, but rather just silently walks away.

His granddaughter is indeed very excited about receiving first communion and often mentions her desire to share in communion by asking "Grandpa when do I get to share the bread?" This greatly pleases Aspot. During the lessons of the required class series his granddaughter never misses even one class session nor a Sunday morning liturgy service while preparing to receive First Communion. Soon father, daughter and granddaughter expect that his granddaughter will get to dress pretty to be blessed and rewarded for her desire and effort.

She like many young Christians has great eagerness and looks towards to the day she gets to bask in glory of God, the attention of her family and the eyes of the entire congregation as she is officially invited into the Church while accepting her very first taste of the 'Bread of Life' as her first very Holy Communion. Yes she is very excited to become a part of the Church!

While the children attend class so do the parents but in different classroom and with a totally different agenda more interesting to adults. Aspot enjoys these classes, even though they are mostly Roman Catholic dogma-centric. He has no any idea about what is going on in first communion classroom but trusts that he and his granddaughter will be informed the day of her First Communion is officially scheduled both in person and by a note in the weekly church bulletin, because it is an important and exciting moment for everyone involved.

Great Distaste

However even while yet, both the granddaughter and grandfather still expect to be informed of the date of the First Communion, a total surprise is made during a Sunday liturgy service when the priest, of Roman Catholic parish church in Black Forest, Colorado, asks the members of the class that received First Communion, the day before, to stand and be congratulated. All members of the entire

First Communion class, but his granddaughter stood. This church actually performed a First Communion church service, a day earlier, Saturday morning without informing his granddaughter or him that they were going to do so.

As the rest of her class stand, with much applause, his granddaughter looks up towards her grandfather with a sudden shock that has not yet had time to feel the hurt. But a second later, tears well up and flow down her face. She quickly casts her gaze down towards the floor, perhaps because she has made to feel like the dirt she sees under her shoes ... Aspot completely stunned, closes his eyes in shame.

The next day Aspot confronts the education director of that parish church and inquires how it is he and his granddaughter both missed being invited to the first communion service this past Saturday. That parish church director raises an eyebrow and cocks her chin out and with a chilling voice says "Well, all of the registered families were notified." And then casts her eyes towards the door as if proposing the discussion is finished and indicating that Aspot has just been invited to leave.

However Aspot now pulls out a chair and sits down firmly in front of her desk. The anger is welling in a fashion that refuses to let him calmly speak. If he could have burned a hole in her head with his eyes he would have. Then after a long silence he simply says "I will talk to your priest and my granddaughter will receive first communion" At which she calmly replies, "You can if you want to, but he already knows the situation and I only have directed the affairs of first communion in the manner I have been instructed".

Aspot is stunned ... but after a quiet minute of utter bewilderment asks "Has anyone ever said 'Do not stop the children from coming to me' ...?"

Then he asks "Has anyone ever said 'I ask that you be one as the Father and I are one' …?"

And finally, before leaving her office, he resolutely qualifies the definitive misalignment of this current condition by quoting "My mother and my family are" … "those that love me" … "who hear my words and do them" …

Spit It Out!

Perhaps Rome knows better than God? We know that Rome makes no mistakes (this is exaggerated mocking, yet) … But then, is it God who makes mistakes …? Well, perhaps God is just a feeble old man? Hey, after all, who wants to listen to an old man, much older than even the hills, when we got a young savvy leader in Rome who knows what we want and need?!

Or, is it possible that we not understand why 'the Son of Man' walked and taught as one of us?

… "slow train" …

Yes, God is old, older than this world … but do we think that Wisdom must obey our beckoning call and maligned dogma?

… "slow train" …

Aspot is red-faced and angry about the conditions of 'The Church' but mainly because its long going divisive behavior seems an impossible problem to ever to be resolved!? "Except for God" and the Spirit of that Old Man, older than the mountains, asks "What have you learned?"

Truth is the Taste Test

With a "Sigh" Aspot releases the table, shakes his head, but looks up and says "Lord, your expectation, of us, is asking the impossible."

From Heaven a voice asks "Do you really believe this?"

No … You ever only speak truth … Nothing is impossible to You.

The very, very Old Man, who is eternally true (holy) to His promises, says "Yes" … "Use the key"

"Nothing is impossible", but let's clarify the issue. We are, at this time, looking at relatively shallow water. Although this 'religion based control and manipulation spirited' mishap, has just harmed an innocent child and grieved the Holy Spirit, it is important to understand that this is but a symptom, of a greater illness, within 'the Church' (the Gathering). Aspot's granddaughter is only one of 'very many' victims of this long-term, on-going illness.

Yes, 'illness' is a reasonably compassionate definition although 'arrogance' might be more correct. An even more appropriate description is 'prideful ignorance'. Before, anyone burns this book, please know that, Love is far more its author than you might think and Love (God) is mercifully trying to move us the right direction. Ultimately, Love, desires we find Life...and His Kingdom …

Got it? Good, let's get moving … So, just what is the 'key' that Love is referring to? What is locked?

Let's change the question; whom is the man, some call 'Christ' who 'born of woman', ate, laughed, cried, walked and taught? What did He show and teach? Did He not say "I came to bring Life"? Did He not repeatedly say "the Kingdom of Heaven is like"? What remains locked …? This question is going to be answered, but first ask why …? One word explains much 'Pride' … But this aged roadblock need not stop any child of God and is <u>not</u> stopping us …

It is so very difficult at times to discern what is moving you, especially when strong emotions, convictions, injustice and impossible circumstances are in the stew … yet strive to "Embrace"

Ok, then it can be easily argued that these two themes 'Life' and 'Kingdom of Heaven' of our Lord and Teacher hinge upon each other but are <u>not</u> the same thing. However, we are all a little different, 'in how we perceive', 'comprehend' and 'develop a full understanding' of any topic. But then Love knows this and continues to help and guide...

So then let us discuss one simple basic about 'Life' because this is the easy to comprehend. The 'abundant life' promised is the potential of our individual spiritual Life, which can and should, splash over our brim with much flavor to our physical life. "He who believes in me", by default obtains Life that is eternal. Now, we go further (find abundance) when we 'hear' His words and 'do' them. Every one of us has the potential to develop a relationship with God/Heaven. In short, all forms of life and Life either grow or die. Each of us 'individually' determine (choose) the growth and eventual final outcome of our own personal/individual life and Life. Got it?

Now "the Kingdom of Heaven" cannot be summed within a short paragraph, but rather, as the Son of Man implies is a 'mystery' that "is like" the many examples He provides to study, comprehend, understand and reach for. Indeed we can reach for the Kingdom of Heaven, because He has shown that 'heaven' is reachable and obtainable by men on earth while also saying "You will see greater things". Before we delve very deeply into this topic let us develop a knowledge basis to where we are headed and to more easily comprehend 'the Kingdom of Heaven'.

Let us begin with a hint directly from His mouth "the powers of the heavens shall be shaken". Notice the He is not talking about a singular heaven but rather a plural 'heavens'. Of similar vein the Apostle Paul, claims to have been taken to a 'third heaven'. In general Heaven is often mentioned in plural starting in the first book of Holy Scripture when it says "Let the waters under the heavens be gathered" So then we will consider and discuss heaven[s]; Are there multiple heavens and if so what does this mean? And again, if multiple heavens, then which heaven(s) is he speaking about when saying 'the Kingdom of Heaven' within His parables? Additionally, we will consider both terms 'Kingdom of God' and the 'Kingdom of Heaven'. Are they referring to the same kingdom?

Now quickly, the very last question asked is the first to be answered; "Yes and No" and "There is only one King". Ok, we see that this answer only asks more ...

The 'Kingdom of God' is purely spiritual and contains only 'good', whereas portions of the 'Kingdom of Heaven' include filaments of both 'good' and 'bad'. Hint; "There is violence in Heaven". The 'Boundaries' of Heaven are at the best vague, until we begin to comprehend, but then much 'grey' will fade away. Got it? No worries, we are only getting started. In the meantime, here is another hint; 'Who will see the face of God but he who has a pure heart and clean hands?" Does any portion of Heaven(s) or kingdom(s) wear any bearing of this question?

Ok, there are actually many basic 'class 101' things we first need to understand before trying to understand the Kingdom of Heaven such as what it means to have 'a pure heart' and 'clean hands'. In other words, we have plenty of preparatory work to do before we try to explore mysteries pertaining to the Kingdom of Heaven.

Firstly, don't doubt for a moment that the 'ruler of the air', Hasatan, has long been doing just what it can do to keep us (mankind) ignorant. Ignorance is a great injustice. Again, we must comprehend, that 'ignorance is an injustice' and an intentional violence to Life. You will hear this repeated numerous time in the following pages as, portions of, ignorance about the Kingdom of Heaven fall(s) from our eyes. Praise God who with compassion helps us see Him ... "Use the key" ...

Stone Faced

Wisdom speaks "Your granddaughter has eaten a dish that is repulsive to Me.", "Tell My sons what I would have them know." ...

"Sons" ... "Sons?" ... "Sons are you listening?" Take back and restore proper care of the bridge ... The King is standing upon the sea" ... "His eyes see, His ears hear, He weeps about mayhem upon the Earth and angered by chaos within His church ...", "The elders dare not hide", "Help elders of 'The Church' find mercy", "Help them stand and speak truthfully while they still have a moment ...", "lest the Judge finds no compassion for their senseless stammer that great last day" ...

Taste This

There are times when it is more appropriate to walk or dance then it is to fight. But as children, it is likely most appropriate to 'sit and listen'. Yet we grow, become sons and then we 'stand' and listen ("a wise man takes much counsel") as we grow into men. Then as men, while still listening and, as most appropriate, we walk, dance or fight. Every good effort is done with Love for Life!

Sons of Righteousness, when will you stand?

Church leaders where is your wisdom? Sons of God are listening ...

God asks His sons to hear and follow His guidance in unity for Life with Him.

Love does <u>NOT</u> cause division!
Faith does <u>NOT</u> cause division!
Obedience does <u>NOT</u> cause division!

Wisdom expects brothers (His sons) to trust Him, meet with an embrace, and work together!!!

8

BLUING THE BLADE

Yes, great injustice is, caused by, a mix of carelessness and ignorance. Yet innocence (not 'carless ignorance'), often stems from, at times 'purposed ignorance', and is a wonderful thing. Innocence allows us to maintain a level of empathy to the needs of others, despite what the world is, otherwise, trying to convince us to do. It is all too easy to become stiff necked and hardened by this world unless we purposefully do our best to maintain some level of childlike innocence.

Love is exceptionally innocent beyond our comprehension. Regardless of His infinite wisdom, infinite knowledge and infinite power, He chooses to remain innocent. This is why when we confess our wrongs to Love and, even but try to, walk His way He fully forgives us and remembers our wrongs no more ... even though He also knows that we will fail, yet, again ... So when we wish to develop a dialogue with Love it is well to approach Him in a childlike manner because He prefers we approach Him in the manner of which one child approaches another. Both are eager to play. ☺

However careless ignorance (not innocence) is pride's companion and one of our worst enemies. The parable of the persevering widow and the corrupt judge is presented immediately after Yahshua (Jesus) discusses the 'Kingdom of God' where He explicitly informs that we find 'the Kingdom' within".

Then, within this same discourse, He asks "When the Son of Man appears will He find faith on earth?" This is an important question ... who knows the answer ...? Why does He ask this question when He has already declared "Will not a builder determine the entire cost of a tower before pouring its foundation?" Who is the Builder? Has He not already poured the foundation? Ok then, when He queries about finding faith we are being invited to understand the riddle illustrated by the corrupt judge parable. This is the Riddle; 'What, despite prolonged forbearance of God, is found quickly?'

Who can understand God's beauty? But praise to our God who loves and gives us the way to find it!

Blossoms of a Cherry Tree

The people we choose as friends say much about where we wish to go. Following is a 'side road' story, which does not directly regard, Aspot's life, but yet offers a well-grounded consideration, which Aspot uses, when needing a reminder about the much good, spread well, throughout this entire world. This story is shared because it is a 'good example of Life' within friends (family), who, being independently, nurtured by Love, yet while also within our sphere of mutually shared influence, indirectly affect our life in some mysterious and often beautiful manner. It is shared because his friend's experience with God is a good example of how faithful and compassionate Love is often found to be. This story is another good example of true life, pertaining to another common person, who is being transformed, and certainly yet within the forge.

Furthermore, this story is a type of break, which is necessary to transition from the experiential portion ("just the facts"), of this book's theme, into 'the stuff' Aspot has been taught ("prepare and wait"). Besides, on a personal note, we are somewhat aware, that Aspot, is become greatly riled and a 'good friend' says he needs, to step back and take, a deep peace-filled breath before he rolls up his sleeves ... to begin ... to finish, a task from an opportunity offered by Love.

Additionally, this side-story also begs being shared as a delightful reminder for the upcoming grandest ever wedding celebration, to which all of mankind is invited, and 'the one' which although, we yet, have no idea when or where it is being held, can be certain that it will be a celebration we just do not want to miss! So now, good friends, let us think 'unity' and "as one", breathe in deeply ... look up ... smile ... and breathe out ... a holy spirited, delightful breeze outward across creation ... to mix with the deepening mist of Heaven ... wrapping tightly about us ...

A young lady, an entrepreneur, life motivated, careless, a mother by age seventeen, does her best to raise her boys well founded despite the fact that their father is a nightclub band musician, who often reserves an inordinate amount of selfish and unaccounted time. His haphazard lifestyle does eventually reveal itself in the disappointing fashion that can be expected from being a handsome musician singing to alcohol influenced women in nightclubs. Perhaps it had been the long sleepless nights in a half empty bed or maybe her own zest for life that prompts her to prepare being able to provide for her boys alone as she takes hold of a lovely conviction, contrary to her own marriage, and arranges a room in her home as an office for her budding career as a wedding planner.

This is a profession that she finds being gifted for doing well. In short time her business has become quite successful. She finds joy in the way her new source of provision allows her to personally interact closely with many excited young couples. For her it was more than just a type of work but rather a service of care. Each wedding is special in some unique fashion and because of her sincere commitment every bride soon finds that they have a personal relationship with her. Likewise she develops good working relationships with service providers based strongly upon shared trust.

Joy from the tasks involved with setting up for the ceremony and celebration of a man and a woman getting married are a big part of her life and motivation. Yet perhaps, there is another element of her spirit that helps spur and provide energy for her daily duties as a wife, mother and business woman. As a child she had watched her father work in his flower-shop and how he displayed appreciation and care for his customers. Even more she watched him read his bible and how he offered help to family, friends and the church they attended.

Although she is, like most children who when, even at their best, only catch superficial observations, she has developed a deep level of understanding between the loving dad she knew at home and the same caring dad she had watched working carefully with the public. However, the craziness of being a teenager, and then, too soon, the arduous duties of a young mother along with the frustration of trying to maintain a lukewarm, if not emotionally abusive, marital relationship have tried hard to strip her of the influence her dad has deeply imprinted within her. Nonetheless, like he once told her, "Every good seed planted in good ground has much chance of producing life. All that is really needed is good soil, light and a little water from time to time."

Late one spring, a wedding she has been planning is quickly approaching. It has been with care that she discovered and made arrangements for exactly what the bride desires everyone's memories to take home with them from the wedding. The plans for this wedding are coming along well and all supporting artifices for the bride's wish about this matrimonial experience are carefully prepared. Now with most invited guests having responded to the invitation and expected to attend, the Wedding Planner is confident every guest will be delighted by the wedding reception wishes of the bride and the much careful detail of this important marital event.

The wedding theme, for highlighting their marriage moment, desired by the bride, is a lively springtime expression based heavily upon many aromatic cherry blossoms. Therefore, long in advance, a large abundance of fresh aromatic cherry blossoms to brighten the wedding hall with a soft pink to reddish pastel glow are ordered, from a trusted flowers provider. It is going to be a lovely, cherry blossom flagrant and memorable gala affair for everyone present.

However, there is a nature of life that allows for the unexpected and this time it is nature itself which marks it's triteness of the moment. An atypically late spring storm drops a hard freeze across the entire eastern half of the United States a few days before the wedding. Her flowers provider immediately gives her a call with a heads-up concern about his obtaining the cherry blossoms from the usual orchards. Yet he assures her that he is going to make sure she has the many cherry blossoms promised.

It is now the day before the wedding and the flowers provider calls her again to let her know that the cherry blossoms have not yet been found. For the Wedding Planner the mild concern is immediately become an unexpected huge issue. Being greatly anxious, she begins to make many calls to every flower shop, but no cherry blossoms can be found. It seems nearly every cherry tree blossom has suffered from the freeze with the only ones surviving are being most certainly reserved for producing a fruit crop.

Far too late, the afternoon of the day before the wedding, she decides that she needs to consider finding an alternative flower presentation but few shops by this time remain open. The overall report from the shops that are found open can offer little more than meager quantities of anything and so even a reasonable substitution for the flower theme looks, at best, very bleak.

Early the following morning, the day of the wedding without sleep, the planner thoroughly distressed, elbows on the table, with her kids arguing beside her and nearly overcome with anxiety about the floral issue, begins to cry. When the phone rings she jumps up hoping some flower shop has found what she most wanted or an alternative which would work. But it is only an old acquaintance that she has not seen or even talked to in years. Although happy to hear a friendly voice that offers a moment of distraction from the approaching disaster, the weight of the flower situation is overwhelming and so her stomach lurches from excitement to strong disappointment when realizing the call is not a good report from a flower shop.

Yet she shows only lightness of heart and chats with her acquaintance for a few minutes. But the need to get off the phone soon and seek a floral miracle is pressing heavily upon the forefront of her thoughts, so the wedding planner mentions that she has an emergency to care for, as a means to put a kind form of early end to this phone call. The woman is quick to surrender the call and say, "Oh, of course, sorry, I must have called at a bad time."

However, there is a short indecisive pause as the caller renders enough courage to continue, "Yet real quick, even thought you might think this weird, the real reason I called is because yesterday while doing yard work I thought of you every time I pondered how beautiful my cherry tree is this year. I just felt like I should call and see if you might have any use for my lovely cherry tree blossoms?" ...

As Measured from the Snow Store in Heaven

Perhaps, in simpler times, when snowflakes were yet regarded with awe and mystery, the soul could be satisfied enough, when catching one on the tongue, to consider offering a thank you to God.

A time when the majority of persons lived in tight knit communities where even the smallest acts of indiscretion would soon be known by everyone so that fear of shame helped establish the standard by which all lived and were held accountable. A time when preserving innocence was applauded and behaving shamefully really meant becoming ashamed. A time when peace and wellbeing were inherent attributes of life. A time when somewhere within the community could be found a place where all could assemble to discuss life and life itself could be heard announcing the sound of a ball yet dropping as a warning, to the careless man, before any tile shattered.

A time when, as a measure of snow was gracefully released from its store in heaven, the hearts of people were warmed while they watched it descend upon their gardens. Simple things are good for Life…

"Good soil, Light and a little water are all Life requires…"

Life: 'How To' Listen

"If I heal the blind then the Kingdom of Heaven is present". Love speaks this audibly, yet Love often announces His presence silently. In all good experiences, whether noticeably active or passively silent, God is present. From these encounters we quietly take hold of a measure of faith. But in general we also ask Heaven and ourselves "What does this really mean?"

We are born ignorant and it is within the Creator's design of Life that our families teach us, as children, the basics. However the basics for Life seem, at times, more than what our teachers understand or is from a set of knowledge 'this world' prefers we do <u>not</u> attain. What we do <u>not</u> know or misunderstand, about a topic, makes the topic difficult to teach or obtain the fruit which the topic offers.

There is an inherent injustice within the realm of ignorance. Lack of knowledge and Wisdom allow harm to Life. Perhaps, more specifically, Wisdom protects Life. The absence of Wisdom, at its best, offers no protection and at its worse is an open avenue for evil. We are going to discuss now some of the lessons pertaining to Life which Wisdom (Love) has been trying to teach us. What is going to be presented is mostly ancient, knowledge that seems to have been misplaced and forgotten across the ages. (Truth will make itself known and re-known regardless of how deep we try to bury and hide it.)

First let us start with what Wisdom has been actively asking us all to understand about life and then we will start to sink our teeth into the Meet'e of Life. First, we should already know that as long as we stay within the 'boundaries of good life', then we are more likely to find joy and enjoy life, because doing so pleases God, is a form wisdom called 'common sense'. For example; common sense directs us to "ask before we take". Our use of common sense allows for a reasonable amount of satisfaction for all parties rather than a shamed spirit and discontent within the community.

As children we develop inclinations as we watch our parents and teachers. In the absence of common sense, we are most often guided by the most common spirit of the culture of which we live. Wisdom lets us know that how we live, upon what standards we base our decisions we either bless or curse our children. Therefore our life is greatly influenced by the type of life our parents, teachers and ancestors have taught us. If we cannot find reason to give a "Thank you!" to those that preceded us, then prayerfully change what we know and teach our children. Give our children's children a reason to be thankful. (Hint: trillions of dollars of debt is <u>NOT</u> a blessing, being handed to any child).

Yes, Wisdom encourages us to upwardly focus on the future, yet also suggests we consider the effects of our actions/inactions yesterday. If we observe our ever changing world it should become obvious that we do not have the capacity to fully fore-guess the outcome of any tomorrow or even the end of this day. At a minimum

Prudence suggests that we follow, or as appropriate, establish, 'common sense' guidelines. It should be no surprise to hear that we need guidelines, because we are human, make human mistakes and know that we can, generally, avoid much unnecessary harm if we stay within trusted guidelines.

Basic common sense is a type of 'guardrail' our ancestors have established by 'listening' and hearing Wisdom explain the truth(s) seen by their mistakes and experiences ... Wisdom ... Let's try to understand what this means ... You see, we have been created with a basic facility of comprehension ('intuition') that helps us hear, understand, through the veil between the physical and the spiritual so that we can be guided towards what is good or best for us at the most basic levels. This facility of basic Holy Spirit comprehension is provided by the Creator, in part, as a 'how to' template for hearing and understanding Him.

As babies, we take hold of our mother's breast by direct guidance from this facility of intuitive comprehension. Yes, even puppies have been created with this basic facility of life, but please do not let this concept cause anyone to get wrapped around the axle. Rather ask why we say "I don't hear God" when He created us to hear Him? Hearing God is key number one and it simply starts by listening to Him, as we are designed, starting early within the womb (yes we do) until the day we breathe our last and meet Him. (This is truth and a basic Life 101)

As children we know how to inherently seek the most basic good by guidance from intuitive comprehension. The sooner we take hold of this basic knowledge, pertaining to language of God, the sooner we can build upon the foundation of hearing Him. It is well for mothers to encourage the baby within their womb to listen, hear and understand that small still voice that is likely, little more than much noise, within the realm of this, wonderfully forming, life. Parents, encourage young children to 'look up' and listen, because, while still very young, they can inherently hear God far better than our deadened ears will allow. If our children take hold of God's language young then who but God knows what their fruit will be. Amen?

Now, common sense is a set of knowledge based upon the use of intuition and what our parents and ancestors teach us. Yes using common sense is very helpful for avoiding pitfalls. But there is another lovely aspect of common sense which, this writer does not know how to adequately describe, yet please bear this feeble attempt. Common sense is also a multi-lingual tool which God uses to help instruct, primarily children, how to better hear and understand Him early in life. We will continue this 'how to' discussion about learning to hear and understand God, for adults, soon within this book. For now, know that teaching children 'common sense' is common sense, especially when we learn how to interpret (ping against) Wisdom's bigger part of it.

For now just chew on this argument; "You know how to discern the face of the sky, but you cannot discern the signs of the times." What was He trying to tell us? Human knowledge alone will not provide the answer to the point we are expected to understand...

Life: "Some Assembly Required"

Ok then, just what is the meaning of Life? This question has been asked by nearly everyone since the beginning of time. (Do not think Love (God) is confused by legal 'sleight of hand' and maligned, politically correct (cursed) definitions of life ... Sigh ...)

The perception of Life being; companionship (a dance) with Love (God) seems a reasonably accurate consideration. Life provides a vantage point by which we can experience the awe, wonder and beauty of God.

Has not every one of us, at some time or another, been caught up within the incredible magnitude and beauty of Creation enough to exclaim "Oh, it would be wonderful to just sit here forever and enjoy the beauty of God" ... Yes, these moments are precious! Yet, although some claim "Life is all about God!" which has a ring of truth, this claim is far from the full truth and worse yet, allows us to rationalize sitting idly and blaming God for the problems in this world.

Yes, we need to relax, in fact, Wisdom expressly tells us to rest. Yes take time to idly enjoy the beauty of Creation ... but not forever ..."There is a season for everything" ... standing ... walking ... Did God not also instruct Adam, the very first man to 'get busy'? Adams first task was to 'name all creatures' which strongly implies that God expects mankind take hold of assigned responsibilities, all of which are centered about 'life/Life'. The true bottom line implies that "life is about us", where the 'us' refers to 'Love (God) and Life (man)'. God is Love and we are Life. Amen? If you think not, that is ok because we are still only warming up ... it sometimes takes a moment to get a nut threaded properly ... patience ... a notch in the key ...

Yes, God gave mankind the task of naming all creatures ... was this honor too extreme to remain innocent? Impatience is a type of arrogance and Adam was too impatient to wait for God to share knowledge at its proper time. Have we (mankind) changed all that much?

When the impact of Pandora's box, seemingly open, takes its full toll of us, then perhaps we will finally learn to become careful about what we reach for?... patiently listen, watch and ask questions...before we take another bite into anything ... test everything, including this book, against Truth.

Although God remains unchanged we did change, when as we (Adam and Eve) tasted the fruit possessing 'knowledge of evil'. We have lost our innocence but God has not. Furthermore we, prove ourselves to, have an unhealthy appetite for the spirit of fruitlessness. Look around ... does it look like we behave on earth as we will when in Heaven? Wisdom provides guidance to Heaven, but do we pay attention ...? Look around ...

Ok, looks bad, but things are not as bad as they (the media) would have us believe. 'Unhealthy fear' is out of ignorance and a tool of the enemy. God (the Master Craftsman) has been with us and we have been making progress. Yes, life is much like the old adage "Two steps forward and one step back" (sounds like a type of dance), but our Master is patient even when we take ten steps back. So then, things are actually quite good, mainly, because 'He is still with us' and we are still learning. He was born among us to teach how to find Life and enter the Kingdom of Heaven ... yes, and we will do it, even while we still breathe ...

Be calm, patient and listen ...

Life is about 'us' (God and mankind). How fast we (mankind) find Life is up to us (mankind)☺. You know what is meant and know that Love (God) allows us to 'choose' what we believe whether it is truth or lies. This condition, established by Love, allows us (mankind) to take ten steps back because He knows that we (the majority of mankind) are sufficiently trusting enough to eventually listen to Love's advice (Wisdom).

In the meantime we worry... we worry because (A.) we have forgotten how to discern what is important ('good') to notice, (B.) we fail to apply good advice ('collective wisdom'/'common sense') provided through our parents and ancestors, (C.) we do not take time to become calm, quiet and listen and (D.) we are too easily misled by charismatic leaders, contemporary idols and fear. We worry because the enemy tells us to... we fail to recall being told not to listen to the enemy... we are too impatient and search frantically to and fro for some scheme to calm our feathers... hey, maybe Rome has an answer...? (Sorry... sort of...)

There is not any law of man (including church canon) that will guide us into either Life or the Kingdom of Heaven. Only Wisdom is the guidance we need to hear and follow. We have come to the end of a season ... now is a very good time to listen to Wisdom... understand this season and why are leaving it...

Seasons... there is a season to plant and there is a season to harvest... Let us comprehend what Wisdom has to say by examining the parable of the 'The Withered Fig Tree'. Some might say "Hey that is only a story". No, it is a parable, enacted in Life by Wisdom... Let's try to better understand it. It is known, by Christ and Hebrew tradition, the 'fig tree' represents the 'tree of knowledge of good and evil'.

The fig tree, like us have good and less than good seasons. But as a general blanket understanding, its fruit represents 'light' (good) and the tree without fruit is likened to 'darkness' (not so good). Just as darkness is simply the absence of light so is 'evil' the absence of 'good'. Therefore, a barren fig tree was conceptually adopted by certain ancestors to represent 'evil'. So then even as Christ walks towards the 'barren tree' ('the Cross') He says, to the barren fig tree, "Let no man eat of you again", but did not explain Himself... He was expressing/ enacting a parable... He is quite literally, reprimanding 'the conceptual evil' which the barren fig tree represents...

"Let those who hear my words... do as I say..."

Seasons... Perhaps it is again time, to listen and learn from our parents and take time to smell the roses... patience... pay attention... we are yet only beginning to warm up...chew on these Words; "Learn this parable from the fig tree; when its branch has already become tender and puts forth leaves..."

Life: Read Instructions First

Our Master refers to periods of time, in His instructions, which use the terms; "the age" and "this generation" for what seems the purpose of synonymous annotation. Because when He says "this generation" He does not specifically mean a fifty year period associated with the cycle of life of individual men, rather He is speaking about a cycle of Life (an age) of mankind across a period of approximate 40 to 42 family generations. But then we should know this because this is average number of family generations between Adam to Abraham and then again between Abraham until the Christ. Hey, how many family generations has it been since Christ? Yes, regardless of whether we call it an 'age', 'generation' or a 'stanza', we have entered a season of harvest at the end of an age.

However, before we grab baskets and trot into the orchard Wisdom suggests we understand what we can expect to find. Just what is the fruit of this age? "Some seasons are good and others not so good." It seems that when we look around we see looting, burning buildings, clubs, guns, new diseases, perversity and death of every form...Is this fruit worth gathering and offering up to God with thanksgiving? Sigh ... It is a little difficult to see the blessing of this kind of fruit, yet Wisdom also asks "When is what we think little too little"?

Does not an orchard contain many trees? So then, let's examine this orchard we (mankind) have planted. First, let us ask, "Is the Son of Man, a man from this same age?" Yes He is. Next let us ask "Did He plant at least one tree seed?"

Yes. But recall that He had already planted the 'Tree of Life', before creating Adam, and it was removed from our (mankind) reach after we tasted the knowledge of evil. But He (Christ) restored our reach through Him and the Tree of Life is most definitely growing close to each of us. Let us, in chorus, raise an Amen and with gusto, gather the fruit made again available this age, provided by the true God and true man ... Life is all about 'us' ... God and mankind ...

But, wait; did He not also plant another tree? It seems vaguely like He did ... Wasn't it a mustard tree or something like that? Yes, there is another tree, allegorically speaking, that He planted, perhaps knowing and intending it needed to wait for a coming age ...? It is doubted that He would ever intend to withhold any 'good' from us, but more likely He knew how a certain type of great good was going to need to be battled towards or otherwise be withheld from us by the 'ruler of the air' ... oh, yes, many have fought for the greater good and progress has been made. Is there not a nation that declares "In God we Trust"?

"Will not the builder evaluate the cost in advance ...?"

"The Kingdom of Heaven is like..." a world with Wisdom and the "Light of Life"...

Let's imagine ourselves amidst a greatly agitated small crowd bearing torches. Our feet are kicking up much dust along with the feet of a person, being partially dragged who has just been caught in the midst of a heinous crime! We demand justice for harm done... to us...? No, but it does not matter, the leaders know a crime has been committed, we are certain someone has been hurt and we demand justice! Hey, look there is a nice stone to pick up and carry along...

Wait, at this same time there is also a large assembly of people, students whom have gathered tightly around a public speaker, a type of teacher. Perhaps we should consider becoming a member of this group, attentively listening with desire to understand what some people claim he offers...? Oops, not enough time to decide because we are in the agitated crowd and even now pushing into and disrupting the larger, quiet crowd...

As these two crowds collide, the leaders, of the agitated group, toss the accused woman, bruised from being dragged, at the feet of the teacher. Oh, the much chaos and noise as these two groups continue to mix amidst a certain amount of shared confusion. All eyes go for an instant towards the teacher, then back to the authorities and then to the woman, who seems immobilized with fear, and sprawling awkwardly, in the much dust, upon the ground.

The authorities speak first, because that is what authorities do and demand the teacher provide advice in regards to the crime committed. All ears quickly perk, as the majority of both crowds sense that the channel has been changed without being told... it seems as though some type of authority, perhaps even a law, is being questioned … but what does this have to do with this particular instance of an obvious crime that has a certain mandate for justice?

Besides, this teacher seems to be avoiding the authorities? He has dropped to hands and knees and is even now playing in the dirt! How strange! Embarrassment is showing on the face of his students. Our eyes go again back to the authorities, for we have become eager to follow them, drag that woman, to the stoning field.

Meanwhile … a sparrow, watches the same earth, of which man is made, being prepared for seed … "Good soil, light and a little water is all it takes" … and with a chirp in harmony to a small still song softly emanating in the spirit of that man on the ground … singing … "Mercy and Truth have greeted each other", "Justice and Peace have kissed", "Truth shall spring out of this earth", "With light of Wisdom from Heaven"

At this time the teacher stands, calmly scan the hearts of many staring at him and without waver speaks "Let he, without error, cast the first stone."

Wisdom … His name … the heart of Love … Life breathes … like wind … into a seed, planted, growing and bearing the wonderful fruit 'Wisdom and Truth' …

Life: the Nuts and Bolts

Look around … something must still be missing … Have we tasted Wisdom …? Do we walk in Truth …? Patience … a key is turning …

The Kingdom of Heaven, or some portion(s) of the Kingdom is (are) wrapped in a shroud of mystery. Yes we know that all 'good' comes from God in Heaven … Yet it is reasonable to wonder about the why and what of that tree in Heaven that bears a fruit, we know all too well is the 'knowledge of evil'...? Heaven is such a mystery... patience... we are getting there...

Earlier in these pages it has been mentioned that Aspot spent some portion of his Life at a monastery in the mountains and while doing so encountered and spent much time with many delightful persons at a nearby Cowboy Church and a teacher named TS.

TS, reminds us that when we read Holy Scripture there are details we might miss because, in part, we do not live in the same time period as when the portion of the Word we are reading was inspired and recorded. This means that it is possible that both we and even the translator(s) of Holy Scripture might have encountered some, perhaps very subtle, handicaps that diminish the full understanding of what the original writer(s) are still (living word) trying to convey (exegesis).

The details missed or misunderstood might be very small but as we know "pennies do add up". Detail is always good when it offers greater insight to a truth. And especially when Life and its abundance might be hinged upon a collective understanding of parents, teachers and the Holy Spirit as they teach and guide us children. Often we use or hear familiar words or phrases, terminology out of context or without understanding what the terms mean.

For instance, recently, a well-educated Christian religion scholar while presenting a spiritual topic repeatedly used (spoke out) described a topic using the term "Holy". He seemed confident that illustrating various items of this topic with much usage of the term "Holy" was adequate and that his students could fill in the void about what the term 'holy' means within the application of the topic being discussed. One of the students listened quietly but could be seen at times to furrow his eyebrows and finally raised a hand to ask what the scholar meant by "holy".

The scholar appeared a bit nonplussed when asked this question and tossed a quick 'you ought to already know, irritated look' back at the student. Is it possible this scholar truly thinks that the term "holy" is a term everyone in his audience clearly understands? Does calling anything holy require no further definition or description? However, this scholar, does reply, but first with a surprised stammer and then looking upwards, appears to be searching for a good definition meanwhile suggesting, if not sloppily tossing out bits of academic rhetoric. After a while he confidently reports "Being holy means being wholesome or whole".

The student who had asked the question, with his brow still furrowed offered a simple nod of his head either to indicate he was willing to either accept that definition or mercifully spare that scholar any further embarrassment. In either case the student seemed to slump a bit in his chair and lowered his head as if to prefer staring at his shoes. It is well that we try to understand some of the common terms we see and use within the context of what we study.

9

LAPPING THE RAZOR

Privately the student later shared that he was disappointed by that answer, but actually more because the acclaimed scholar failed to show any deeper understanding of a subject of which he is a supposed expert. The fact that he had not presented any new light to the already commonly vague understanding, of the specific topic, is not itself a problem but might be a symptom of a real problem within some strains of industrialized Christian religion where it has been observed that some Christian leaders appear to prefer pacifying the flock with obtuse generalization rather than possibly offending anyone.

Let us ask; Is it better that we allow ourselves to be pacified rather than helped towards a better understanding? Well, there is no simple answer but in general it seems that some of us consider the Truth from the Word of Life as being just too burdensome and tedious, so with carelessness choose a more meager form of existence and at times even make formalized complaints about the political incorrectness of the more energetic and honest teachers.

Furthermore it has even been suggested that some of the larger institutionalized religions purposefully keep the deeper meaning of scripture vague and encourage us to believe that scriptural topics are just too mysterious and deep for anyone but the church leaders to understand. Therefore by this method the leaders of churches secure their roles. This thought is a bit too nefarious and conspiratorial than this pen is willing to fully accept but rather suggests that men in general prefer to be lazy whenever allowed. This includes both those who choose to lead and those who allow being guided. Both are noble roles but both require some amount of effort and perhaps the greater effort required is to actually speak up when Truth and Life are <u>not</u> found coming from the pulpit or the perceived teachers.

Nevertheless, it has been actually heard and written by some scholars that they believe that interpretation and understanding the Holy Scripture should always be left only to the clergy because it is beyond the realm of understanding of the flock. Well, we, the under-educated, feeble-minded flock, should be careful about following any strange personal interpretation of the Holy Scripture, but this scholarly statement is pure ignorance, if not arrogance, and contains a certain lack of faith in regards to the obedience of the Holy Word and purposed will of God.

All terms in scripture do have specific meanings which we can understand and should earnestly strive towards being able to use for describing our own demeanor and lives. There is much reason to desire casting off every gray area and all muddiness of understanding about anything that affects how we walk.

Do we ever hear God (Love) trying to guide us? Why is it that many, if not most, believers, who sincerely trust guidance of the Holy Spirit, struggle for the guidance they seek? The reason varies greatly and individually. Yes, we have been advised to ignore the ever present noise, which comes from many sources, including the enemy, but in general we are our own worst enemy. Just too busy, to rest and listen. Yes, Wisdom, instructs us to rest, for a day, at least once a week… just for this reason? God is willing to talk with us, but we generally fail to hear and accept the dialogues we are offered to enter.

But even when we have locked the enemy outside and have forced ourselves to become quiet our next biggest problem is that we fail to think like the Holy Spirit does in work and speech. As, part of the solution, it is well to know that God does <u>not</u> 'idly speak'. Rather when He speaks it is for a specific purpose. Perhaps the purpose is only to say "I love you" but there is a purpose to every word of God. He speaks often but, in general, we are not well enough acquainted with His voice or dialect to even realize that He is talking to us.

This takes us back to the basics and the 'common sense' which comes from our facility, of intuition. By helping maintain the collective knowledge known as common sense we are helping work towards the specific purpose of learning to hear and understand through intuition, which ultimately teaches us how to hear God. Of course we have His Word as the guidepost reference to 'ping what we hear or think we hear' against. Likewise, it is well to become periodically quiet at times every day and consider how we are walking at that time. Are we getting anything/anywhere from/with the lessons of life?

When Aspot had noticed the two dollar beer sign in front of that dark striptease joint, this was most certainly a test and he knew it but chose to enter that joint and that is when the lesson began. We are all somewhat different, yet generally, when we see something that excites us we just reach out and quickly grab regardless of whether or not the head of it is attached to a snake. Why do we do these things to ourselves? Well it looked good on TV didn't it? How many lemmings does it take to, screw in a light bulb hanging beyond the edge of a cliff?

By the way, God (Love) is the author of good humor and if we pay attention, it is not uncommon, to feel a wind of levity within His, 'good father' corrections (guidance) to the mistake(s) we are making. Furthermore, He uses humor to help us feel where we are at with Him, despite the gravity of some errors we make.

Lessons ... There are reasons why God tells us to gather and pray, one of the most basic is that "two heads are better than one", but then, that is just common sense.☺ Our numbered voice is louder and He can speak, to many, so that, at least, one person might hear an answer. But, in general, it is just often more productive to ask a companion to help hash out and understand the explanation, that might be coming from Heaven. Sigh ... There are reasons He calls us to gather and one of them is because He does truly call some people to shepherd His children. We most certainly need basic guidance and true insight through family, friends and teachers who can pass on words from Wisdom ... Wisdom ... Oh, so very hard to find ... why?

In the absence of wisdom, let's, at least, roll up our sleeves and punt ... we are, at this time, discussing 'hearing God amidst the lessons' ... more specifically we are challenged in life with lessons that puzzle us, mainly because we don't even know the basics that should have continued being taught as they were two thousand years ago. Politics … Sigh … it seems politics are more entertaining … sigh …

We largely do not hear God and obtain Wisdom because we fail to know a few simple basics … push politics aside and listen … What are the basic of life? Do we clearly understand them? There are standards of behavior which guide us towards an abundant Life, the Kingdom of Heaven and Perfection of Life in the Spirit. In fact the teacher TS teaches; there are three basics and they are 'Holiness', 'Purity' and 'Righteousness'.

The teaching of TS are important, to God, because He made sure that the teacher (TS) and student (Aspot, this writer) crossed paths, in a remote mountain location, by unlikely series of circumstances. Therefore it can be claimed, that Love (God) is literally "Teaching, every man, in all wisdom, that we may present him *perfect* in Christ Jesus". As an aside, please know that TS has been taken Home and so, it can also be said, Love alone leads the lesson that follows:

TS put much stress into the importance of Holiness, Purity and Righteousness. But these attributes follow understanding some fundamental basics, 'Obedience', 'Faith' and 'Love'. Obedience, faith and love … these three are the primary 'categories', actually spiritual attributes pertaining to perfection in Life. It is helpful to understand how these individual (primary) attributes, although separate categories, do work together to achieve better spiritual and empirical behavior. We are going to study how these attributes individually help align us with, Holiness, Purity and Righteousness as often used in Holy Scripture.

Some of this material we should already know because it pertains to basic Life. Yet some of this material seems to have been misplaced in the back of the cupboard and overlooked far too long. The nice thing about treats from God (Love) is that they never get stale! Yippee, look what has been found in the cupboard! Abundant Life!

Life: Abundance

Mankind is granted the opportunity for possessing a richness of life in a far greater sense than any other creature. Quite frankly, it is doubted that man can fully comprehend, this greater state of wholeness, fullness, liveliness, keen awareness, the infinite extension of man's capacity for having a presence in every aspect of being in both the physical and spiritual realm, life. "I am come that my sheep might have life and that they might have it more abundantly".

It is well to be intimately cognizant about and dutifully careful to attend life because God offers fullness of life, "God is eternal life", as further annotated by The Word with descriptions such as:

"Light of Life"

"Breath of Life"

"Bread of Life"

"Water of Life"

"Wellspring of Life"

"Fountain of Life"

"Newness of Life"

"Grace of Life"

"Promise of Life"

"Word of Life"

"Spirit of Life"

"Instruction of Life"

"Way of Life"

"Book of Life"

"Crown of Life"

"Prince of Life"

"Savior of Life"

"Resurrection of Life"

"Tree of Life"

These titles are provided as hints and outright declarations about how we can benefit and obtain Life, in the manner, His providence always intends the entire Book of Life (Holy Scripture) to help guide us towards.

Life, our life, our children's life, the life of our communities are important enough that He was willing to humble Himself, be born, walk, share, laugh, suffer and die with us so that we might be able to feel and comprehend the greater hope He offers in a tangible, approachable, obtainable and very human kind of way towards Life.

Yes, our physical life is limited by the manner our physical body dies, we know we are still expected to care for it so that we might enjoy this life and encourage our children likewise. Yet man has been given a distinct privilege, not known possessed by other creations, the capacity to defy death in the form of a spiritual life that continues after the mortal body dies.

"I am come that my sheep might have life, and that they might have it more abundantly."

Abundant Life is 'wholeness' of a person's being. God is the ultimate source of all elements of Life and when we capture the abundance offered to us, we also have some measure of access to the infinite resources of Providence (God). With this fact in mind, we can begin to realize just how immense, unfathomably abundant Life can be should we become virtuous, perfected enough to be called by Love His sons! Being holy is just one attribute of Life that men being perfected are most certainly taking in their hold.

If we go without pleasure in our spiritual Life while we walk as mortals on this earth, how much the less satisfied will we be when we lose our physical body and wear only the spiritual? But this we already know. Life requires good ("All good comes from Heaven") decisions, choices and becoming wise in Love and Life. Knowing this and choosing Life is the core of Wisdom and the heart of Love.

i) Perfection of Life

"Therefore you shall be perfect just as your Father in Heaven is perfect." Our Lord is telling us, in essence, to become "God-Like" in our life. Therefore we should desire to aim for an understanding that helps us align our mind, heart and strength with the Holy Spirit's guidance and the only perfect man (Jesus). By aiming our life this way we will come ever closer to a spirit growing within that agrees ever better with the Holy Spirit and therefore Love. It is much easier to find God present in our life when we live in a fashion that is more like Him. In short it becomes easier to dance when we begin to understand how to dance.

The only perfection of Life mankind has seen is the Lord Jesus (Yahshua). After all He is the only perfect example; was born, ate, walked, worked, played, sang, danced, laughed, cried, tempted, breathed, died and lived

162

very much like the rest of us? Yahshua (Jesus) is truly a man just like all of us. And He proved that we can be perfect, in God's eye, by His example. The Holy Word instructs us to, likewise, achieve perfection. Yes, aiming towards perfection, in this world, is difficult, but He has shown that it is possible. Perhaps His desire for Life is a perfect type of motivation for us?

So just what do we know about the only perfect man Jesus? For starters God is not careless and we can be certain that the parents He selected to birth and raise His Son were carefully chosen. Our Lord was born into a Hebrew family of devout Jewish religion orientation and died upon the cross a devout Hebrew man. Joseph had been positioned and purposed by God to help provide and care for Jesus and was much older than Mary when they were betrothed. We have reason to believe that Mary was given to God when she was very young and lived in a type of convent until she became of age (about the age of fourteen).

We also have reason to consider and believe that Joseph was a carpenter ('Master Builder') which is a Hebrew term applied to both carpentry and scholars of God. Joseph was a widower with grown children of whom James the Greater was one of them. This means that James is an older (step) brother of our Lord and it is this same James whom doubted Yahshua (Jesus Christ) until after the Resurrection but also the one whom excited the first council of the disciples, held in Jerusalem. The sons of Zebedee, James the Lessor and John (the teenage disciple whom laid his head upon Jesus breast (the Holy of Holies)) during the last meal, were sons of Yahshua's older step-sister Salome. Therefore James and John were actually nephews of Yahshua. These considerations add minor insight into the greater family environment of which Yahshua grew up within and some of the disciples with which He walked with during the most active part of His ministry. Family is very important in the general strategy of the Master-Builder (God).

Family ... God created the family unit and this structure suits His purposes well because a healthy family unit is a form suited for the development of children into men that can be further trained and perfected by God. This is one reason why the enemy of mankind continues to destroy the family unit and proper parental formation of children that is expected of us by God. Yahshua (Jesus) was born and raised in a spiritually healthy fashion of a devout, tight-knit, well manner family.

But 'a family' can be and is often bigger than just members living within the same confines of a family home. For instance, we know for certain that John the Baptist jumped in the womb of, his mother, Elizabeth upon the greeting of Mary, the mother of God, and is the cousin (family) of Yahshua. The healthy family unit is very important to God (Love) for the benefit of mankind.

TS believes that, it was common for, Hebrew people of that time had a good understanding of what God regards as acceptable child formation which leads towards perfection of the spirit, behavior and wisdom of a man. This understanding reflects some of the terms most commonly used in Holy Scripture. In short, a perfect man (Jesus) possesses three attributes of person that greatly affect his attitude, behavior and beliefs. These three attributes are 'holiness', 'righteousness' and 'faithfulness'. These three terms have different meanings, but bound in nature through our relationships with God. Or in other-words they should be spiritually intra-linked in a manner that leads to Life. But what does these 101 basics of Life mean?

To answer this question we must first establish what it means to seek a 'goal'. Holy Scripture instructs 'be perfect'. Therefore being perfected in the Spirit is one of our goals. Perhaps being 'perfect' is just too ambiguous and far reaching for us? It shouldn't be. The reason it might be is only because we are not taught (ignorant of) what being perfect meant and still means to Jesus (God). Any goal that is not defined cannot be understood, reachable or obtainable. Is not this statement correct? Once again, any goal that is not defined is not obtainable.

Setting a vague or an undefined goal does not allow us to clearly know how to begin or end the search. With a little explanation every man will see that with sincere effort perfection can be accomplished to a degree acceptable to God. And while doing so, we find Life and not just Life, but as our desire for Life strengthens and becomes bolder, we also find the abundance our Lord promises. Let us remove the obscurity of scriptural terms so they no longer are like carrots dangling from a string in front of our nose that we can never quite reach.

Let us start with the term 'holy' which, that, one well-educated Christian religion scholar off-the-cuff defined as "being whole". Ok, we know being 'holy' is important because the Word instructs us to be holy and therefore we know it must be important for Life. However before we accept the wholesale "being whole" definition, let us personally examine what we know about the term 'holy' and try to develop an in depth understanding of what it means to be holy, as a necessary element of Life.

First, 'holy' is a very common term often found in scripture and it must be asked why any scholar of scripture cannot immediately provide a solid basic definition? Isn't it a bit bizarre that such a common term in a topic of great importance is not thoroughly understood by the majority of believers?

Well, if "being whole" is what it means to be holy then it is without much effort we quickly realize that "being whole" can mean a whole lot of things. Firstly the term "whole" is defined in a dictionary as: "Comprising the full quantity, amount, extent, without diminution, all parts included, undivided, entire, full, total …" This definition continues in a lengthy cluttered fashion and when all is said and done, being 'whole' simply suggests being part of the 'whole enchilada'. Therefore, being whole might also mean being an active participant in let's say the city of which we live. Typical cities, in 'the whole', have churches, homes, children's beds, beds under bridges, bars, stripper joints and so forth.

So let us consider beginning our day by attending at least one or more churches, join the crowd in a café for lunch, perhaps follow the whole crowd down to the tavern for pool and beer. But wait don't forget; to visit the gym for exercise, a massage, a movie and the ballgame. Whew, being whole might take a whole lot more time than you can find in your whole day! In short "being whole" only implies being whatever is preferred and offers nothing towards knowing how to find Life as intended for mankind by God.

Yet, 'being whole' can pertain to every fashion of living/ existence in this world of every fashion. Holy Scripture says "There are many gods' and therefore "being whole" can pertain any of these many gods if it is the primary foundation of the term 'holy'. This writer does succumb to the fact, it seems, that every type of religion possesses some type of 'holy man', and agrees that 'holy' is a term which can be used in a general 'any godliness'

Therefore to the extent each person is subject to their god they can claim a type of holiness. So then this city is most likely full of holy persons. For example, those whose god is drugs, the inserting of a needle is then a type of holiness and being whole as they do their own thing and just be themselves, nothing missing in how they include all parts of themselves, their inherent and adopted attributes. Perhaps in this case being whole and holy can be dangerous to the point of death.

Ok, to be fair, the context of which this scholar was speaking was inherently understood by everyone, present at that time, to mean being whole in some Creator (Father, Son and Holy Spirit) Godly fashion. But then what does this vague comprehension mean? Can the common man ever hope to be Creator Godly? We are a mixed and often confused people of different persuasions and personalities who often, even non-intentionally, choose to honor and show reverence to our own favorite god.

Simply put, the manner in which Holy Scripture applies the general term "holy" is much better described as "being a whole lot less" and is one very good example of the adage "less is more". This leads us to the fact that the first five books of the 'Old Testament' within the Christian Holy Bible are called "The Wisdom of God" by many scholars and especially those of the Hebrew religion. The term holy is generally understood, by the Hebrews, to pertain to a form of sacredness stemming from being "set apart" and many Christian scholars also accept this as an appropriate meaning.

However, this is a 'far too comfortable' description, in part because it is yet obtuse and distant enough for most of us to easily and complacently disregard as not applicable to common life. God is not instructing only hermits in a cave but rather He is most certainly instructing everyone, which includes the common person to be 'holy'. Yet, there is also an element of truth to the association between 'holiness' and being 'set-apart'.

It is not by coincidence that an apple "set apart" from others in the barrel ages more gracefully than apples tightly packed. And we have certainly heard it said "A single apple can spoil the whole bunch", and this saying is a great opening for how to proceed. A perfect apple is firm, juicy, tasty and appealing to the eye, without spots of infirmity. An apple that gracefully ages, simply shrivels as the moisture of its youth evaporates, leaving it possibly as hard as a rock, yet still eatable, with seeds vibrant and able to reproduce life.☺

Yet even the apple sitting alone on the counter, too long, will ninety-nine percent of the time become good for nothing but the trash bin. Why is this? It is because they become rotted following attacks from parasitic spores found in the environment. The apple will remain whole until the tiny spores which land upon it begin to slowly eat at it.

You see, fruit and mankind's natural minimal defense system needs an adequate amount of exposure to the sun (son) for protecting 'the seed' and for nurturing 'future generations'. The fruit, by design, requires sunshine for proper aging. We likewise require a graceful type of 'passing on the token' aging process which also requires an appropriate amount of sunshine. This is again part of the '101' minimal level of understanding and therefore we need not focus on this because this is something we should already know very well.

Let us rather put much attention to the dynamic, and at times extra, effort God expects of His creations during their troubled times. Apples generally tend to become infirm quicker when maintained in large groups rather than when maintained alone. In fact it is nearly impossible to let a bunch of apples gracefully age and dry out together. But one by itself can be seen to gracefully age. The apple is no longer strengthened by the tree, but it is still very much alive and by Creator design tries to defend itself using inherent defense mechanisms. Part of the reason for this is because the pushing from the weight of others cause bruises which weaken an area of the apple and causes it to become less able to naturally resist a mold attack. However unchecked mold in dark, damp, conditions grows in strength and soon defeats the best resistance of even non-bruised apples.

So then if the built in defenses provided for its youth diminish, how then is it possible for any apple in a barrel to remain whole? This is in all cases, an unlikely long-term condition when buried in a barrel. Yet the whole barrel can be slowed from rotting if the apples which develop rot are swiftly removed from the barrel and this is because the spores of mold are themselves quite weak. For us this might mean easy adjustments to our life, such as ignoring that two dollar beer sign outside the strip joint.

Yes, removing ourselves from 'the barrel' is a common behavior of persons being led to holiness, but 'set-apart' is really only an indication of some 'holy' process that is taking place and not the correct definition for either 'holy' or 'holiness'. In fact, it takes more holiness, to live among others, and still walk with God, than it does to live in a cave.

It has been said "Holiness is not the absence of sin, but rather the presence of God". There is much basic truth to this claim which we will try to better understand, but keep in mind this is only part of the full truth about holiness. So, what do we know about ourselves that might allow and encourage the presence of God? Being holy means, in part, being within the presence of God but this is also true for the other two most primary attributes of a perfecting man with Life in him and aiming for the Kingdom of Heaven.

The prophet Moses instructed the Hebrews to set the first born animals apart for God. However, let us ask, "Does the act of setting the firstborn apart make the firstborn holy?" No, man cannot make anything holy. Even consecration rites are but a prayer (request). Rather it is only God's blessing that establishes 'holiness'. Yet, God asks us to be holy and therefore we (everyone) are expected to reach for this blessing. However 'Holiness' is not an idle or static condition and God expects, as we reach, for this blessing that we understand our task/role and either have or are asking for the Strength and Wisdom to "do" it.

Again, the natural resistance of the apple against mold is by the Creator's design a type of action performed by His will and is therefore a type of obedience. We also by nature have a minimal built in level of defense called our 'conscience'. Therefore our minimal defense against lures of the enemy follows our willingness to hear our conscience and effort to "take all thoughts captive". This is minimal obedience of the Creator's design and therefore the Creator.

Love always encourages us to improve our 'natural' resistance to attacks of the enemy because the enemy continues to change its tactics. For us to sit quietly 'on-the-counter' and think we can continue to defend ourselves is carelessness. For us to be living tightly packed 'in-the-barrel' (city or similar) without continuing effort to strengthen our resistance against the enemy is catastrophically reckless.

Be certain that we do have one Creator who has always known that how, at times, we need to duck if wishing to avoid being hit by the enemy and therefore He has applied similar design principles across the board for all of His creations including even tree that bears the apple and the human that bears the son. Yes we are both designed to continue our species by procreation. This 'procreative' category of creation is inherently provided appropriate degrees of comprehension to allow us to quickly adapt to the environment for the purpose of continuing the cycle of life.

For instance the apple tree if finding the season to be exceptionally dry will put its energy into the growth of additional roots for ensuring that it can bear fruit following years, if not the present one. The apple tree comprehending the conditions of the environment and applying itself accordingly, displays a behavior for preserving itself in a fashion that leads to being fruitful. This is a type of obedience to the design of the Creator and therefore to God. In fact we should be able to see that basic procreation obedience to our Creator is a fundamental expectation by God of all creatures.

In a similar fashion future parents generally try to be prepared for the care of their forthcoming family. If possible they will, in advance, possibly get an education, but most certainly get a job or already have some manner of providing for the needs of a family. However, even if the conditions of their earthly life are adverse, some amount of consideration for the life of their children is always considered before and while the wife is carrying new life within her.

The Holy Word declares "the bed of a man and his wife is holy". What does this mean? Well, foremost it is a minimum obedience of the Creator to procreate! Therefore it can also be said that the bed of a man and his wife is an obedient bed (environment). Ok, but again, there is nothing man can directly do of himself, including the act of procreation that makes anything holy. Rather, in this case, the resulting conception (miracle of life), is the blessed holy gift from God. So then it can also be claimed that, our obedience, to perform the act of procreation, leads to holiness.

Applying effort towards fruition of any portion of God's will is always a blessed form of obedience and therefore a type of holiness. For example, when parents spend time with their children, teaching, guiding and loving them these are holy times of the family. Children watch their parents to discover their most easily reachable future skill potential by simply observing their parents in action. The father or mother should be willing to include one or more children as they work their own chores because this benefits the child with a lesson of life. This taking time to teach our children is another minimal sacrifice of obedience acceptable to God.

Grace filled time, with our children, provide helpful, illustrated demonstrations that nurture Life and are necessary nutrients, vitally important to the family. General obedience to Life is certainly 'blessed behavior' and a type of grace filled holiness. We can easily achieve this level of holiness, but the key to understand is that holiness stems from being obedient to God. When we perform any task, He wills, then we perform a task He blesses and therefore we are performing a holy task.

Just as a good father teaches his children to cook for the benefit of their physical life so he does also for the wellness of their spiritual life. The minimum expected obedience, in respect of, the very real gift of spiritual life is accordingly elevated. "I have set before you, life and death, blessing and cursing: therefore choose life, which both thou and thy seed may live"

Ok, then why do we call 'Holy Scripture' holy? It is holy because it is the inspired word of Love (God) and The Word never returns void which implies that it never fails to perform its task. Therefore the Word is obedient to Himself (God) and the task performed by the Word is performed by God and therefore directly Holy. The Holy Word always delivers the intended message regardless of whether or not any listener accepts the message, as presented by God speaking through His prophets "so it is with the word that goes from my mouth: it will not return to me unfulfilled or before having carried out my good pleasure and having achieved what it was sent to do"

10

TESTING THE BLADE

i) Holy, Holy, Holy

Being holy simply means being blessed in obedience to God and His Word. A holy action is an action or effort extended that is in obedience to God (the Father, the Son and the Holy Spirit). Holiness is an attribute of Life, for which we should reach. Obedience to God leads to holiness.

So then when we read "God is holy" does this mean God is obedient? Yes, that is exactly what it means. He is obedient to His Word (Truth) and that is the bottom line. God is obedient to His promise to Life to the extent that He lets those who do not have Life, hang him on a cross, so that they might feel His mercy and begin their search for Life.

In general Holiness is a Godly attribute that man can obtain and is a necessary element of Life for working toward a Godlike type of perfection. 'Holiness' is only one element of the three most basic Godly attributes which are 'Purity' and 'Righteousness', as discussed below.

By the way, the description "being whole or wholesome" much better aligns with the full meaning of "abundant Life" which comes from finding a Godly Life that includes Holiness.

ii) Purity

Holy Scripture describes Abraham as a man of great faith because he was willing with single-minded (pure) trust in the purpose of God to climb a mountain and go the full extent of an incredibly difficult task assigned by God. We can easily acknowledge his trust in God as a pillar of faith. Yet faith although absolutely necessary for any relationship with God, by itself accomplishes nothing observable. The epistle of James claims that faith alone is little more than a reflection of a man's face in a mirror. Because Abraham walked up a hill and tied his only son "whom you love" to an altar of stone in obedience to God, Abraham can also be known as holy. Faith in God and obedience of God are two of three most basic attributes of perfection in a man's Life.

God is sovereign and moves as He pleases, but God is Love and Love considers Life within His every move. So then, what was it that prompted (tested) Abraham to the extreme extent of binding his son, Isaac and raising a knife to kill him? Was God testing Abraham? No, this action of Abraham followed rather confused beliefs that came, in part, from the environment of which Abraham was raised and is what tested him. But God allowed Abram's test, because it offered much learning for a man that God knew He could trust and loved dearly. In part, this test provides mankind with much insight including "by God's mercy we learn to fear Him". If nothing else this lesson reveals the potential strength of 'pure' and possibly even 'blind faith'. Faith is a powerful thing and should be applied with care.

In part, because by a portion of the Wisdom from this test, Abraham and the rest of mankind are enlightened, by how we are shown that pure faith, of any god, <u>can</u> be contrary to Wisdom and Life.

More importantly, perhaps, this test informs us very clearly that a good relationship with Love requires a pure heart, steadfast, strong unwavering which is only found through faith that has come from God. Love (God) strongly encourages us to find faith and thereby possess strength, endurance and perseverance because Love loves Life. Life will falter, fall and fail without God and Godly strength. Faith is the basis of real strength, is a basic attribute of every man being perfected and faith is always a gift from God.

However, even though God seems quiet, more often than not, He often offers gifts and it is always well to be watching for and ready to accept them. Watch and expect the gift of faith. Be expectant. Our Lord, Yahshua (Jesus) told us that all good comes from God. This is a truth and it is good ☺ to trust in Wisdom. Once we take this truth to heart we begin to notice much more attention from God. Anything that affects us in a good way can be considered as coming from God and worthy of a "thank you". Even very small good things are well to take notice. Even the small gift of faith which comes along with the conviction and belief that "all good comes from God in Heaven" will continue to grow if we but consider even the penny, on the ground, a good gift from Heaven and say thank you when we pick it up.

We are likely to miss the big gifts, from God, if we handicap our ability to notice Him by ignoring the many small gifts Love provides for us. Each little gift we perceive as good is from God so if we take a fraction of a moment to acknowledge Love as the gift giver then along with each small gift from God there is also a measure of faith to take hold of. When the traffic light ahead of you turns from red to green as you are still approaching, does this not cause you a flash of uplifting? Well for many of us it does and therefore even this very small good thing deserves some amount of thankfulness.

All such small things felt as being 'good' are worthy of giving thanks to God. Find value and be thankful for all the many tiny gifts while we wait expectantly for a surprise of much greater. Faith is like the carbon slowly being absorbed into iron within the heat of the furnace. This type of carbon is where Life finds resiliency, temper, perseverance and strength. Life is worth taking thought and effort to absorb. Breathe it in!

Faith if followed leads to 'Purity' in the trust of God's purpose. Purity in Love's (God's) purpose offers the strength of God! Purity of Heart in God's Purpose is further referred to here as "pure", "pureness" or "purity". 'Purity' follows faith. Yes by faith alone are we saved, but by faith alone, 'Purity' is not found ... Hold on, take a deep breath ... we are getting there ...

Where did Abraham find his massive measure of faith? We do not know the details but we can be certain that his faith came from God. Without doubt Abraham was quite observant and willing to accept every offered gift of faith. He most likely watched for, gathered and took firm hold of each small measure of faith as God provided it for him. He remained increasingly expectant of God in every situation he encountered. It was this expectation which rewarded him, with no great surprise, when three strangers he treated like royalty turned out to be from, if not literally, God.

Abraham in his faith had trust in God but also had a gross misunderstanding that came from having lived amongst strange minded people. This misunderstanding was about Life after death which was inspired by God within him but misaligned by his rubbing elbows with a people who made blood sacrifices to idols.

God speaks to us individually in a manner which allows our personal knowledge about any topic, to help us understand Him. Obviously at some point God and Abraham were having a discussion about Life after death. But Abraham still did not fully understand what he heard about this mystery. Yes, Abraham did get some of the truth correctly. Life after death required a sacrifice of blood but he did not comprehend that Life is spiritual and that no man should take life to find Life!

We are fortunate in that we can read the text and have a rear view mirror, 20/20 view of Abraham's lesson. The comprehension of mankind to the dialect of God continues to improve but it is still easy to misunderstand God. This is, more often than not, because we insist on speaking like humans and seem to avoid learning the 'God Speak' dialect of Wisdom.

Very rarely is Life an island of one man and in this case we know that Life includes descendants as numerous as the stars. Life … Abraham … Yahshua … us … Love remains consistent, persistent and present. We can believe that Abraham was going through a continuing process of becoming perfected because we know that he had a relationship with God (Love). Obviously Abraham has faith in God and God knows this. Abraham is obedient to God and God knows this. But what do we know about Abraham's ability to know and show love?

The recount of his greatest test does not show how Abraham loved his son, Isaac, even though God explicitly tells Abraham "your son whom you love". Was it necessary for God to tell Abraham what Abraham already inherently knew or was this really a question for Abraham's conscience? We know that Abraham was quick to let his wife be mistaken as being his sister so that she was taken, not once, but twice, by kings of lands through which he travelled. This fact makes it possible for us to consider that God although knowing the incredible faithfulness and holiness of Abraham still had some doubt about Abraham's capacity to understand the wisdom of Love. It seems that Abraham quite likely had a significant deficit in the needed understanding of love and therefore was missing Wisdom.

Ok, but didn't Abraham love God? Well this is not explicitly described in any fashion within the recount of his great test. But then what exactly does it mean to love God? Even when we say we love God what exactly do we mean? Do we truly love God? Are we sure? What does loving God mean? What does love mean?

We only know 'love' by how God (Love) has shown us examples of love. In all cases He shows us love, in some understandable fashion that benefits life/Life (us). We can honestly say we love Jesus, largely, because of the love He showed us. Much of our understanding about love comes from many generations of mankind having continued to read and study these examples. We can say we love God by the many ways He has promoted the lives of others before us. As children we watch our parents and others and mimic what we learn from them. God has long been showing mankind what love is by how He has ever continued to bless our lives often in many wonderful ways. So again, when we show someone 'love' it is only because God has been teaching us what love is.

It is very possible that Abraham loved God but if so it is still not evident in Holy Scripture that Abraham treated his family in a fashion that shows very little, if any, 'wisdom of Love' and therefore we are allowed to doubt, wisdom of Love, by the recorded life of Abraham.

God is Love! Godly love has wisdom. Would Love (God), looking forward towards the mother of our Savior, not be trying to perfect the linage of the family and the Life of which He has purpose to birth His Son? Of course He would and still is. This test of Abraham brings the missing wisdom of Love to the surface for Abraham to ponder and ponder greatly and his lesson is also for us to ponder and ponder greatly.

So did Abraham develop the wisdom of Love? We can see hints of wisdom in Abraham's linage but we can also see much "stiff necked" behavior of his future family members as well. Yes, Jesus (Yahshua) is a member of Abraham's linage by being the son of Mary. So we do know that God (Love) humbled Himself to walk as a man and show us perfection through, a form of, Abraham's lineage. Nevertheless, it seems that mankind, in general, is perhaps a little slow and still shows much evidence of failing to get the message. And thankfully we yet remain in a continuing process of being perfected by Love, towards His good purpose.

iii) Righteousness

Ok, what do we know about, the only perfect man, Jesus (Yahshua)? Well for one, we know that He was righteous. During a recent bible study (fellowship) the verse "He allowed being baptized, fulfilling all righteousness" was discussed and someone asked "What does it mean to be righteous?" A priest said that in this instance it means 'Respect'. A deacon said "It means obedience" another person said "He did this out of faith" and yet another person said "It means that He started fulfilling His mission in the world". A student simply nodded his head and said "Yes".

If the teacher TS had been at this fellowship he probably would have remained quiet unless asked what he thought and then would have most likely said that all the previous answers were, at least, partially correct but then would have proceeded to say that 'love' is a better answer, because it is having love in our heart that leads to righteousness. Ok, respect is a form of love but does not hit the center of the target. Then he would have explained that although 'love' is the primary ingredient to righteousness, righteousness is not possible without Love (God) and requires an appropriate portion of 'Holiness' and an appropriate portion of 'Purity'.

Then the teacher TS would have scanned the room to study the light in the eyes of everyone present, would possibly sigh and say righteousness is only part of the story in this verse. Yahshua is righteous but moreover He is a perfect man and we can see righteousness in what He has shown us. We must ask what kind of righteousness does this verse pertain; is it the righteousness of God or the righteousness of man? There is a difference between the two although less or more than we might think.

This verse is about the wisdom of God (Love) and it shows the righteousness of a true man as purposed by His baptism(s). It also shows the righteousness of God when we understand what this verse means. This scripture is about baptism in shallow water but it offers a whole lot more depth into the greater wisdom of God (Love). Yahshua (Jesus) is a man and He is very well aware that He is a man. Jesus walks like men do simply because He truly is a man. Yes, Yahshua's father is God in Heaven and Jesus is privy to, an extent, the intimate will of His Father. Yet, He was formed in the substance of earth, born and walking, 'with' us, suffered and/or rejoiced 'exactly like' us and truly a man.

Let's examine His baptism by water, while considering the fact that He walked across the barren landscape of Israel, to be at the Jordan River for a purpose ... a purpose of men ...

1. Jesus (Yahshua) makes an arduous journey to the river to mix among a large crowd of believers, gathered to seek God. This gathering is caused out of a stir in the Spirit and because many believe that John's purpose and mission is inspired and moved by God. This effort of everyone, within this crowd, is a type of 'obedience blessed by God' and therefore this action of all persons present is 'Holy'.

2. Yahshua allows himself to be taken hold of by the Baptist, submerged beneath the surface of the river and lose access to breath and potentially life. This act is 'faith in the strength of God' which itself shows strength of conviction. Every member of this gathering agrees within the same trust, bearing the same strength and 'Pure' in their unity with the Spirit and each other.

3. Yahshua has also come to this river to encourage His brother (cousin) John. This is love. Furthermore, his humble submission to the Baptist before many witnesses, shows respect for John's holy assignment which is an 'expression of Wisdom', or in other words a 'Righteous' action.

Jesus (Yahshua), a man, is Pure in spirit, with unwavering faith, Holy in blessed obedience and Righteous in how his life, even to the last drop, is an expression of Wisdom. Only Christ, the Son of Man, the King of Peace and Conviction is perfect enough to force death to kill itself and thereby also effectively and affectionately re-grant access to the eternal Tree of Life.

John (the Baptist) is obedient to Love (God) and his assigned task in Life. This is holiness. John is motivated, in part, by single-hearted faith (Purity) in God (Love). Additionally, John's mission is an expression of the Wisdom of Love and therefore righteous However, John is not perfect. Let us all work towards the perfection of Jesus (Yahshua) but be satisfied if we can get even a fraction as close to being perfected as John the Baptist.

Life: Perfection

Obedience serves God's purposes and leads to holiness ... A holy man is obedient to and blessed by Love. Holiness is an obedient heart strengthened through faith and guided by the wisdom of Love. Holy actions should be carefully governed and guided by Righteousness and strength found in Purity.

Faith is a gift, unwavering trust and expectation of God ... A faithful man with Wisdom is obedient to Holy tasks made possible through the providential strength of God (Love). Always beware that 'blind faith' can be reckless and without Wisdom.

Love (the noun) is gentle, love is kind, love is humble, desires Life. Love is Wisdom ... A righteous man walks with Wisdom. Righteousness is an expression of Wisdom made through holy (clean) and pure hearted men. Righteousness is an expression of Wisdom by a holy action, with strength in purity of heart.

These three attributes, (Righteousness, Holiness and Purity) work together and when applying an appropriate amount of each it becomes possible to approach perfected

Life and reach into the Kingdom of Heaven. However … it requires a gathering to enter the Kingdom of Heaven. Patience … we are getting there …

The 'perfect man' outline is a helpful tool that accurately illustrates, in a simplified manner, the goal our Creator has established, for us, which is Life. It is intended to help clarify what we already know in a way that it can be often considered, understood and used to help set achievable goals. In general the perfect man concept provides guidelines towards, perhaps better understanding, and emulating the perfect man, Jesus so that we might together ever more find the abundant Life.

Perfect Man Visualized

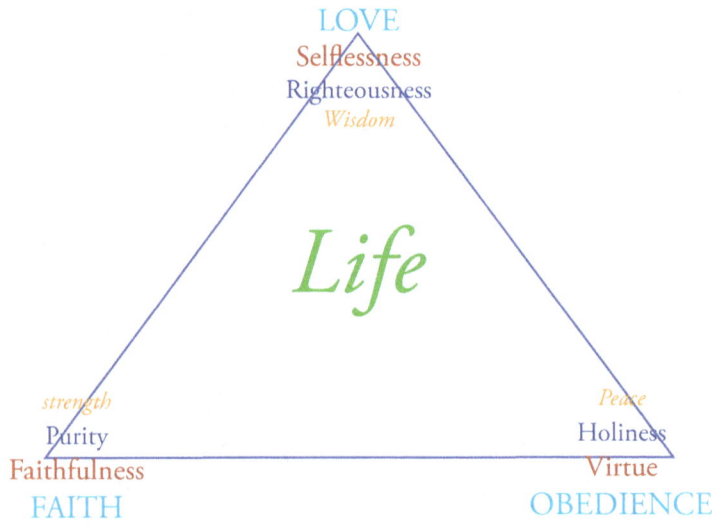

Would it have been necessary for God to come to earth and walk with us if we had been patient, trusting and obedient enough to allow Love to teach us what we need to know in the Garden of Eden? We might never know. But we do know that Love is reasonable, compassionate, merciful, faithful and holy and why because Love continues to show us these things. Mankind is learning the dialect of Love.

Time has no hold on God, so in similar spirit we can watch Jesus even now greet John the Baptist with but his ankles only just being wetted within the Jordan River. Many things, in our time, have happened since this moment and which have either brightened or dimmed our spirits. We reflect both what our ancestors have reached for and what we even now reach towards.

Let us remain cognizant of the meaning of the fulfilled righteousness of Yahshua (Jesus) and the death defying extent to the meaning of baptism. God has humbled himself to show mankind what we need to find Life. Just as His life was a journey with a purpose in the will of our Father in Heaven it is well we walk out our Life with God, the man Yahshua, starting as young as possible, which is common sense, ever intending to defy death! Eternal Life is the great fruit and fulfillment of righteousness.

Now keep in mind that righteousness is a selfless attribute of a perfected man. Therefore we do not aim to become righteous so that we might consider ourselves righteous because if we do we will never find righteousness. Rather aim for the wisdom of Love and the abundance of Life and when you find it, your righteousness will be silently observed and inspire others.

Remember righteousness, as has been explained, is most heavily based upon love but it does require an adequate amount of both faith and obedience to be perfected and effective. Holiness is achieved primarily through walking obediently but also requires an appropriate mix of love and faith. Purity is primarily through the gift of faith but requires an essential amount of unwavering love and obedience.

It is possible to be obedient but not be holy but rather even offensive to God when our behavior is lacking in love or faith. Being obedient does not necessarily mean being righteous or pure, nor do lovely expressions mean they are holy. Understanding what it means to invite God's presence is the bottom line for becoming and being holy, pure and righteous. The greater mix is important because it leads to a level of perfection which shows sincere desire for God's presence.

Perfection follows an intentional balancing of the three primary attributes within our spirit. By developing an appropriate ratio of all three we find shades of greater spiritual perfection such as being merciful and compassionate. Each of these and many others are important within the overall nature of perfected men and ultimately the perfected gathering in the Kingdom of Heaven. In general it is helpful to know that each of these greater attributes is heavily based, or perhaps more accurately, achieved by finding Life with an appropriate mix of love, obedience and faith.

11

WHILE THE DAY IS YET TODAY

O k, then, Love provides helpful guidelines but what do we can and should we do with them? "Take My hand!"

When Love calls out "Take my hand" do we think that His request is so that we can pull Him, from the fire? Of course not, but then on the other hand do we think that God wants to do everything for us? No! Love does not work that way. Rather when we hear Him say "Take my hand" we know that he expects us to 'engage' into the issues and work with Him so that our Life and the Life of everyone about us might be improved towards abundance and His Kingdom.

Yes He shows us the way but with the caveat of expectation "Those who hear my words and do them". Our Lord has always shown us 'the Way', not in a demanding manner but rather through lovely guidance into Life. He helps 'us' tend to the growing of good desires within our hearts. These are the personal persuasions that benefit our corporate goals that start individually within. We can only find peace by focusing upon the situations within our hearts.

When we get a tire caught in a mud-hole and begin to spin, it does NOT improve the situation by stepping hard on the gas. Nor does it help to have someone else to do all the work (the guile of governmental assistance). We generally should more often rely upon local solutions and think for ourselves! Let off on the gas and allow the tire tread to take small, slow bites and ease ourselves out of the pothole (common sense).

Consider others... Let us start with our family. It has always been of great importance for parents to spend quality time with their children in order to produce and raise a quality family. If we take time to play and yes work with our children and yes even our spouse then family life improves immediately and dramatically. Yes we are all busy people, but rushing around and not taking time with family will cause far more damage than what our 'rushing around' thinks it is going to gain.

Truth is fruitful. Perhaps in the lapse of truth we have Hollywood to guide us? Here we go again...plodding along "dup-de-dup, dup-de-dup..." like a herd of cattle being fattened for slaughter...

Let us think about the problems of today for a minute. Everyone is going to have a different list based upon the priorities and what they are currently struggling through at home and their political disposition. But in general if we really consider the important issues, they are for the most part based upon the biggest problems inside our home, which includes our children, marital struggles, finances. Then our list should also consider the political issues of our country and our community. Most likely you will see that the major issues are some form of human life and inter-relationship related concerns. Yes our lifestyles are greatly affected by technology but it is NOT technology that is the center of the individual issues. Rather, there is something more personal that needs to be addressed. Got it?

Yes, the tone, of problems, is ever changing but, in general, the basic problems remain the same and have for thousands of years. The core of the main problem is that our culture and family starve for peace. We will never find peace in the latest technology, the biggest bank account or the highest seat of importance.

There is a reason why God (Love) expects us to rest with Him at least once a week (preferably the Sabbath which is the seventh day). Aspot encourages taking one day a week regardless of whether or not it is Saturday (Sabbath) and spend rest time with God, our families and friends. Rest people! God strongly expects us to. Read how the Hebrew people were repeatedly reprimanded when they did not take this much needed rest. Gather together...visiting a church is a good step forward...

If we want to fix our problems in society it starts with us fixing our relationship with God. We are speaking about wisdom people. We do not require religious experts to explain wisdom because only Wisdom itself can. In fact it is doubtful mankind is capable of understanding and knowing but very little in regards to our incredible God. Therefore, let us stop spinning our tires, calm down, take notice of the basic way to Love and things will get much better, because we will find peace in our heart and home if we do. And when we do this much we will also begin to make much better choices. The issues of today will resolve themselves without a whole lot of worry once we improve our intra-personal relationships, mindset and the corporate goals based upon Wisdom.

Ok, but how can we know or come to possess any measure or God's wisdom? It is wisdom to desire God's presence but there is an ordered progression of seeing this desire become fruitful. First, take hold of even the smallest gifts offered by Love with expectation (faith). Even mercy is a gift. It is written "By the mercy of God we learn to fear Him" It is also written "Fear of the Lord is the beginning of wisdom". It is Wisdom that provides us the type of desires to hope for. The Psalmist tells us "God gives us the desire of our hearts". What does this mean but that Wisdom inspires Godly desires within us. And then as we walk with God (Love) these desires do become fruitful. This is the kind of fruit we truly do want, because it is, in part, His fruit through us and it is Life.

Family, Love and Truth

Life starts with a well-grounded family (Good Seed Planted), Love (God) and Truth (Water).

We are a purposed tip and have the well positioned capacity to be an effective edge. He has provided us the liberty of planting our own fields and making our own beds and by our choices decide how effective we might be and whether Life or death is our master. Therefore let us look at our self in a mirror and ask "Is Love within me?" For those of us who are not sure, this ('right now') happens to be a very good time to find and embrace Love and listen to Wisdom.

There is purpose. Love does not wait forever.

12

BEFORE SUNSET

We 'The People' are granted many choices. Look up and choose wisely people.

We have approached a new stanza in the song of Love. This book, motivated through a whisper from Love is imperfectly recorded by an imperfect man. Nevertheless, always take hold of good, feel Loved, find 'Abundant Life', seek greater Truth, harmonize in every next stanza and expect to see Heaven…yes even as we yet breathe…

Aspot wishes everyone God speed,

With Love,
Aspot

PS (hint); Heaven is multi-tiered, 'spiritual' and 'physical' realm, accessible to all mankind. The veil is very thin … test the key … Wisdom shows us how to use it …

www.ingramcontent.com/pod-product-compliance
Lightning Source LLC
Chambersburg PA
CBHW071736120626
46550CB00002B/548